Argentina's Angel

Copyright © 2007 by Diogenes Verlag AG, Zurich,
as *Als ob ein Engel*. All rights reserved.

Translation Copyright © 2014
by Edward Larkin and Thomas Ahrens with the permission
of Erich Hackl and Diogenes Verlag

All rights reserved. This book or any portion thereof
may not be reproduced or used in any manner whatsoever
without the express written permission of the publisher
except for the use of brief quotations in a book review.
Printed in the United States of America

Piscataqua Press would like to express its appreciation to the
Bundeskanzleramt in Vienna, Austria, for assistance in
publishing this book.

Interior photo: Statue at Holy Cross Cemetery. Calumet City,
Illinois. Copyright © 2010 Eric Pancer. Used through
Creative Commons 3.0

The cover picture is used with the permission of the
Tenenbaum family.

ISBN 978-1-939739-23-0

Published by Piscataqua Press
A project of RiverRun Bookstore
142 Fleet Street
Portsmouth, NH 03801
603-431-2100

info@riverrunbookstore.com
www.riverrunbookstore.com
www.piscataquapress.com

Argentina's Angel

Erich Hackl

Translated by
Edward Larkin and Thomas Ahrens

Piscataqua Press
Portsmouth, New Hampshire

To the real peacemakers of the world.
May success be theirs.

Acknowledgments

The translators would like to thank Paul Larkin for his help in creating the cover; the good people at Diogenes publishers for their support of this translation; Malcolm Willison and Janet Gold for their careful reading of the document; Tom Holbrook of the Piscataqua Press for his assistance in preparing the manuscript for publication; and the author, Erich Hackl, for his encouragement and support.

Translators' Introduction

I

How would we respond if we found ourselves living in a society permeated by state-sponsored military aggression against political dissidents? Would we toe the line, or would we seek to resist the dictatorial measures? Erich Hackl's *Als ob ein Engel. Erzählung nach dem Leben* (Diogenes, 2007), which we have called *Argentina's Angel* in our translation, depicts the response of one individual. Gisela ("Gisi") Tenenbaum, the daughter of left-leaning, secular Jewish parents—Helga Markstein and Willi Tennenbaum who left Austria as children just after the *Anschluss* in 1938 and married in Buenos Aires in 1951—chose to contest the oppression. Frequently characterized as angelic by those who knew her, Gisi, the second of the three Tenenbaum daughters, was born in 1955 in Mendoza, Argentina. An excellent student and athlete, Gisi had a keen sense of social justice. Coming of age in the 1970s at a time when the military dictatorship had seized control of the Argentine government (March 1976) and the 'Dirty War' raged, Gisi eventually joined the Montoneros (*Movimiento Peronista Montonero*) and became a fierce opponent of the injustices and neoliberal economics of the regime. While representative government was eventually restored in 1983, Gisi was among the 8,000 – 30,000 Argentines who were 'disappeared' in the years 1976 - 1983.

Gisi is typical of Hackl's heroes and heroines, who are real people opposing social injustice and political oppression in a variety of historical contexts, e.g., the National Socialists in Germany, Franco in Spain, the Uruguayan dictatorship, among others. Literally translated, the German title would read "As if an angel. An account *after* or *according to* life." Indeed, the story of Gisi's life is told some thirty years after her life had been ended, but, more importantly, it is an account that is based on well-researched historical documents, conversations with friends and family members, relevant letters, and finally well-considered supposition. In the end these sources form a tapestry of varied perspectives that tries to capture Gisi's character and the times she lived in. As the *Berliner Zeitung* has observed: "For Erich Hackl, reality is far more absorbing than anything he could ever imagine. He is a writer who lives — in the literal sense of the word — with the characters of his books."

II

The recipient of numerous awards, Erich Hackl was born in Steyr, Austria in 1954, and now lives in Vienna and Madrid. Among his other books are: *Auroras Anlaß* (*Aurora's Motive*), 1987; *Abschied von Sidonie* (*Farewell Sidonia*), 1989; *Sara und Simón*, 1995; *Entwurf einer Liebe auf den ersten Blick* (*Narratives of Loving Resistance*), 1999; *Die Hochzeit von Auschwitz* (*The Wedding in Auschwitz*), 2002, and *Die Familie Salzmann: Erzählung aus unserer Mitte (The Salzmann Family)*, 2010. His most recent work is *Dieses Buch gehört meiner Mutter* (*This Book Belongs to My Mother*), 2014. Known for his documentary style of narration (perhaps literary non-fiction best describes his preferred genre), Hackl has been translated into twenty-five languages. *World Literature Today* summarizes his writing as follows:

Erich Hackl's concise and hauntingly dense works of prose have gained him a huge audience and great success. At the bottom of his efforts are usually some forgotten beings, victims of our century's cruel history, with their authentic albeit not exactly remembered biography. Here Hackl, the Austrian author, overly sensitized perhaps because of his own country's extreme insensitivities, steps in and tries to bring about an act of belated justice and redemption. This obviates the question whether Hackl is a fiction writer or a historian, a lawyer of the 'small people' or a missionary voice of human dignity: he is all of these, and ideally they all add up to make a writer.

III

Hackl's prose is unembellished, unsentimental yet highly empathetic. Given his evenly-paced, sober style, translating Hackl might seem an easy task. But the deceptive subtlety of the author's lexicon required many creative solutions. Our work was further complicated by the author's preference for elliptical constructions. Rendering them into a fluid American idiom while retaining the ellipsis presented numerous challenges, and we hope we have succeeded more often than we failed. Furthermore, the orality of the text presented complexities. The text may have been written to resemble the documentation and conversations that lie behind it. So it is not surprising that at times Hackl's writing seems to read more like a loosely connected series of conversational sentences than polished paragraphs. And passages that might seem more appropriate in the past tense sometimes appear in the present. For the most part, we have kept the present in those situations as they emphasize the simultaneity of the writing and the interview. Moreover, Hackl generally does not use quotation marks when his characters have something to say. Nor does he take pains to explicitly indicate who the speaker is. (This is especially true in his *Wedding in Auschwitz*.) By and large, we followed him in these matters, trusting the reader's investigative skills to determine who is making the comment. Similarly, occasionally a pronoun is ambiguous or the referent occurs in the sentence after the pronoun. Usually, we left this to the reader to decipher as well. Such instances of uncertainty reflect the thematic uncertainty—Gisi's ultimate fate—of his study. The orality of the story can also be seen in the frequent run-on sentences. On occasion, we revised these constructions, thinking they are too unique to German to be translated adequately as run-ons in English. Finally, Hackl is fond of anaphora, the repetition of initial phrases, as they bring a lyrical and dramatic quality to the writing; we have followed him in this regard as often as we could.

Given the loose structure of the story, we supplied chapter titles that indicate the location and the rough chronology of the events. We have used footnotes sparingly, only when we thought the allusion might be too foreign. In the end, our translation, which eschewed any systematic theoretical paradigms, represents one more effort to keep alive the bravery of those who opposed the totalitarian authority in Argentina, and elsewhere.

Edward Larkin
Thomas Ahrens

About the Translators

Ed Larkin is a professor of German and the Humanities at the University of New Hampshire. He holds a Ph.D. from the University of Pennsylvania and has published on 18th, 19th and 20th century German and Austrian authors. He has published translations of Friedrich Schiller, Erich Hackl, and Eugenie Kain.

Thomas Ahrens is a teacher, translator, and artist working in Berea, Kentucky. He studied English and French at the Free University of Berlin and holds a Ph.D. in Germanic Studies from Indiana University Bloomington. He has worked as a translator of business, scholarly and literary texts and published on the German author Horst Bienek.

We have previously collaborated on the translation of Leo Perutz's *Between Nine and Nine* (Ariadne, 2010) and Erich Hackl's *The Salzmann Family* (under consideration).

Possibilities of a return? To
what had been?
　　And advanced only a couple
of steps?
　　Catch up
　　Catch up
　　now
　　right away

Johannes Bobrowski

"In eine Hauptstadt verschlagen"
("Ending up in a Capital City")

I

I wish this story could end like a fairy tale: "The door sprang open, and their daughter entered the room with her golden hair and her luminous eyes, and it was as if an angel had descended from heaven. She walked over to her father and mother, embraced them, and kissed them. This is just how it was; they all cried for joy." In fact, it was different. Gisela Tenenbaum ("Gisi") did not return, and what remained was a tapestry of voices, some tightly woven and others threadbare and frayed. This tapestry bears the stamp of truth. This is how it was; this is what we experienced. Her parents say this; so do her sisters and her friends. They have grown older since then, some thirty years and more. Only Gisi remains as young as she was, twenty-two, and half of her future now lies behind us.

II
Mendoza, Argentina
1977

In 1977 Good Friday fell on the eighth of April. It is highly probable that that was the last day that Gisi was alive. It is certain, however, that she spent the night before in a small, sparsely furnished apartment on Calle Italia in Godoy Cruz on the outskirts of Mendoza, Argentina. Eight hundred meters above sea level, the city was founded in 1561; it was destroyed three centuries later by an earthquake, and subsequently rebuilt with wide boulevards, bordered by plane trees and jacaranda trees, and included squares, flower gardens, and a large park, which, like so much here, is named for the South American freedom fighter San Martin.[1] In 1817 the General and his army set out from Mendoza to liberate Chile and Peru from colonial rule. The city nevertheless is rarely associated with rebelliousness; its residents are considered conservative and reserved.

There are three of them in the apartment: Gisela Tenenbaum, José Galamba, and Ana María Moral. They are Montoneros, isolated, in need of help; their leaders are about to flee to Rome but not before affirming the prospect of a quick victory over the dictatorship and calling upon those

---

[1] José Francisco de San Martín Matorras, also known as José de San Martín (February 25, 1778 – August 17, 1850), was an Argentine general and the main leader of the southern part of South America's successful struggle for independence from Spain.

comrades who are to remain behind to display even greater determination and redoubled vigilance. Perhaps the three intuit their defeat, but the extent of their catastrophe is not yet evident; there would still be no way out even if they knew exactly how things stood, that the military were on their heels, that they had no choice but to continue the fight, to persevere, and not abandon their comrades. Moreover, they recall the feeling that they have pursued a just cause with strength and confidence. They have known each other for a long time; they have faced great danger together; they have given each other words of encouragement and consolation.

It is unlikely that their living together in such tight quarters (two rooms, a hallway, one bath, and a kind of laundry room) further tests their resolve. Ana María and José are active in one cell, Gisi in another. She leaves the house on the morning of April 8, 1977, to attend a secret meeting of her group in Las Heras. A little later the other two also leave the ground-floor apartment. When they step outside, they immediately see the special forces sealing off the street. There are plainclothes policemen, armed, sitting in three or four vehicles, delivery trucks and passenger cars (Ford Falcons). José and Ana María take each other's hand, as if by chance, and then take off down the street, past the houses. Ana María goes to the left, José to the right.

The men are surprised and for a moment uncertain – Who should run after whom? Should they try to head them off? Six or eight seconds pass before they take up the chase. José hears the piercing sound of gunfire. Next to him the rear window of a parked car shatters. He sprints down the first cross street he comes to, past an old woman, a cart, and a fruit seller, who quickly disappears into a doorway. Hidden by a truck, he crosses the street and then turns another corner opposite a bus stop. A bus is just pulling out. José jumps on it, and, panting, falls into the seat behind the driver.

He escapes, unharmed, evades some checkpoints, and finds a hideout somewhere in town, for one night, for three nights. Then he is able to get out of the city, with or without the help of some strangers, and hides in a forest. Two months later he gets a message to Gisi's parents, asking if they could help him. Willi and Helga hide him in the trunk of their car and take him home with them, knowing that the police could show up at any time. A few days later they find him a place to stay in a remote brick manufacturing plant, with Daniel Romero, the brother of a union worker. The following year the military will finally track him down and haul him away along with his employer and his employer's brother. None of them will ever be heard from again.

Ana María makes it to the Church of Nuestra Señora—163 Joaquín V. González Street—where in her desperation she seeks refuge. As she tears up the steps to the door, the cement shatters with bursts of machine gun fire. Suddenly she feels the powerful impact of a bullet to her back and stumbles. She falls over the threshold into the church where the priest is getting ready for the afternoon services. Instead of attending to the wounded Ana María, lying in front of him on the stone floor, beseeching him to close the door, he goes outside and signals her pursuers. He is anticipating a large crowd of churchgoers on this day when Jesus Christ died and when Ana María will die "from severe anemia caused by an acute loss of blood" according to the clinical report filed by Dr. Alcides Alberto Cichero, the military doctor who reported that the death occurred at 8:30 PM. She will die in the church or on her way to the hospital or in a prison cell under her alias, Graciela Beatriz Luján.

Between six and eight o'clock in the evening Gisi's older sister Heidi catches a report on television that describes the most recent success of the security forces: a woman believed to be in her mid-twenties is said to have died in a fire fight with the security forces when they were executing a search warrant in the Department of Godoy Cruz. According to the authorities the apartment served as a secret operations center for the insurgents. Weapons and subversive flyers were said to be found in the apartment. A camera pans across the smashed furniture and the clothes strewn about on the floor. Heidi stares at the TV screen, hears the jarring voice of the news anchor but refuses to accept the certainty that this is the apartment where Gisi lived. She informs her parents.

III
Vienna, Austria
1930–1939

Helga Markstein was born under a lucky star. She begins the memoir that she wrote for her grandchildren a few years ago by describing the circumstances of her birth: a hot summer day outside Vienna in Stadlau, in the Neu-Strassäcker housing development on the left bank of the Danube, her mother's labor pains on the morning of June 29, 1930, and the joy and disappointment of the invited relatives because Fanny Markstein, instead of serving them schnitzel, potato salad, and cherry compote for dessert, gives birth to her second child in a Viennese hospital at noon, a baby whose appearance was exactly what her brother Heinz had demanded—blond and blue-eyed. To make sure, every evening Heinz had placed a lump of sugar at the window as an incentive for the stork, who in those days was responsible for the arrival of children.

The family lived in a whitewashed row house. The kitchen and living room were on the ground floor while the parents' bedroom and those of the two children were in the attic, at the top of a steep staircase. Behind the house was a large garden with fruit trees, bushes, and vegetable beds. Helga played there with her favorite cousin Peter; during the week her father, Rudolf, left the house early in the morning and was greeted joyfully by his young daughter upon his return in the evening.

Rudolf Markstein, said to be a man of good judgment, worked in the accounting department of a publishing house that published two leftist newspapers, the *Neuer Wiener Tag* and *Die Stunde*, and he did not hide the fact that he had socialist leanings himself. But the workers' revolt in February 1934 caught him by surprise as he sat in his office in Canisiusgasse in Vienna's ninth district; he was only able to get home after the fighting had subsided and his comrades had been defeated. A few days later Rudolf was arrested: an aggrieved neighbor had hidden a rifle in the Markstein family's compost pile, and, as he had intended, the weapon was found during a search of the Markstein residence. The city was under martial law at the time and the illegal possession of weapons brought the maximum penalty, but Rudolf Markstein had a good reputation, and several influential friends testified to his innocence. Some shots had also been fired in the housing development; Fanny Markstein lay down on the floor with her children so that they would not be hit by a stray (or intentionally aimed bullet) fired by police officers. Then she sought refuge with acquaintances in a town just outside the city limits. Helga was not frightened, but she did miss her father. If he were there, no harm would come to them. Even at that time he had wanted to leave, to emigrate with his family to Australia, but his wife resisted.

Freedom has had its day, and the Nazis continue to get stronger; look what's happening in Germany.

Come on, it can't get that bad.

When the German army marched into Vienna in March 1938, the adults were sitting by the radio, quiet and depressed. Helga did not know why they looked so serious, but she understood that danger loomed. Will my dad and your dad have to go to war now, she asked her cousin. Susi shook her head no, so Helga felt relieved. But in June, a few days before her eighth birthday, some men came to the house and took Rudolf and his brother away. The following night, loud voices, harsh laughter from the street, and then gasping and rasping outside the door. A drunken Nazi had climbed up the ivy to the bedroom window; he wanted to scare the hell out of that Jewish Markstein woman, but a rafter gave way under his weight. As he fell, he was lucky enough to grab two tendrils, and holding onto them he slid down into the garden. A neighbor who had been alerted by Helga's mother's cries for help chased the intruder off with a pitchfork.

There were not many people in the development who continued to be helpful and friendly; most of them just avoided the Markstein family, no longer greeted them, or even regretted that Stadlau was still not free of Jews. The mailman left letters at the garden door, first from Dachau, then from Buchenwald. I am healthy; I am well. Then, overnight, they had to abandon their house. A great-aunt took them in; her apartment in Döbling was not far from the *Hohe Warte*, one of Vienna's well-known small hills. Beginning in September, Helga and her cousin were forced to attend the primary school that had been designated for Jewish children. The classes were wildly overcrowded making normal learning impossible. Adolescent Nazis often loitered in front of the school, and occasionally they would attack the children. Helga was alert, but one day some boys surrounded her and shoved her up against a wall. Fortunately, a man in blue overalls saw what was happening. He pushed the boys aside and threatened to beat them if they did not leave the girl alone. Helga's knees were still shaking when she arrived home.

But the incident did not prevent her from strolling through the streets with her cousin Peter in the afternoon and marveling at the magnificent villas with their richly decorated façades; in the display windows of a toy store they took in the numerous toy automobiles and horse-drawn carts, the steam engines, the construction sets, and the dollhouses.

The adults meanwhile stood in line at the consulates hoping for a visa, for each of them and for the two men in the concentration camp. Thanks to the efforts of a relative in Buenos Aires, who owned some land in Bolivia and contacted the authorities there, they finally received their exit permits to emigrate from the German Reich. In January 1939 Helga's father and her uncle were released from Buchenwald, and in the early morning of the first anniversary of the German occupation of Austria the Markstein family boarded a train to Hamburg at the West Train Station in Vienna. A few weeks later they arrived, exhausted and penniless, in La Paz, Bolivia.

IV
Mendoza, Argentina
1977-1983

Helga and Willi saw Gisi for the last time on April 3, 1977, Palm Sunday, which they spent together in the mountainous region of El Challao, a popular destination for day-trips, eight kilometers outside the city. They returned home to Mendoza around seven o'clock in the evening and dropped Gisi off near the apartment in Godoy Cruz. Before she got out of the car, she made a date with her mother for the following Sunday. The two of them ordinarily met at a bus stop on the busy Paseo de los Andes at the corner of Armani, where Helga pretended to be waiting for a bus. Several minutes later Gisi would show up and walk past her. Helga would usually follow her into a café, where they could talk undisturbed and without fear that someone would be eavesdropping. But on Easter Sunday Helga waited in vain for her daughter, and again a week later. In the meantime she learned that the military had been informed about the time and place of a meeting of the underground in Las Heras and had ambushed ten or twelve Montoneros whom they overpowered and kidnapped.

Nevertheless, Helga and Willi continued to believe that Gisi had somehow managed to escape, and they had some reasons to be hopeful. For one, they noticed that their house in Calle Coronel Díaz was still under surveillance. Every night and often during the day, they had observed two men sitting in the front seat of a car parked on the opposite side of the street. They were apparently keeping an eye out for Gisi. If she had in fact been captured, then there would have been no reason for them to maintain surveillance of her parents' house.

Moreover, toward the end of the month, a young man who had studied with Gisi at the technical college, came to Willi's medical office to ease his conscience, as he assured him.

I knew what was going to happen. That Gisi would be caught. But I did nothing to prevent it.

Not knowing how he should react to this unexpected confession, Willi ignored it and made a vague hand gesture. But he would have liked to ask this student several questions. From whom did you learn that Gisi was in danger? How could you have helped her? And why are you telling me now that you could have helped her? Perhaps the young man wanted to pump him for information. Perhaps he was just waiting for Willi to say that he should not reproach himself, their daughter was doing well as far as they knew. Then the young man would have had reason to believe that Gisi was still in contact with them. Who knows whether this might have been a ploy to catch Gisi.

There was yet another piece of evidence suggesting that Gisi had not yet been captured. A few days either before or after the visit by her former classmate, another young man, also one of Gisi's classmates or fellow students at the university, stopped Willi on the street.

Guillermo, can you believe that I saw Gisi the day before yesterday in a vineyard on the outskirts of town?

Are you certain?

Absolutely.

Did you talk with her?

He said that there had been no opportunity to do so; he wasn't alone at the time and he did not want to endanger her or himself.

But it was her; I recognized her right away!

Willi and Helga knew the young man to be serious and reliable. He certainly did not want to deceive them. It is conceivable that he in fact had made a mistake. Or perhaps that Gisi had been captured only later, in the beginning of May. At that time Helga and Willi held out some hope that they would see her again. They believed that if Gisi had not yet been arrested, reporting her missing would only have done more harm than good. That's why they waited so long to report her disappearance to the court, by means of a motion of habeas corpus, which of course was denied.

Once, again in 1977, an acquaintance told them she had seen their daughter in Maipú, in a pharmacy. Gisela was said to have gone into the store, had a prescription filled and then left.

That's how it was; I swear by all that is holy to me.

In any case they never heard from her again; she was the kind of person who would have done everything to get a message to her parents; in this regard she was always very dependable. Today Helga is convinced that Gisi had already fallen into the hands of the military on the eighth of April, at the meeting of her group, or at the latest in early May.

Five or six years later a nurse with whom they worked on an aid project in a poor neighborhood in Rivadavia approached Helga excitedly. After hugging her, she whispered: I have great news for you; you won't believe it. She claimed to have heard two doctors in *Hospital Central* in

Mendoza talking about the many people who had disappeared during the dictatorship and about the agonizing uncertainty of their families. She then said to them, I have two good friends, their daughter has also disappeared. One of the doctors asked what their name was. Tenenbaum, she answered. Well, he said, of course, Gisela's parents.

Tell them not to worry. Gisela is in a safe place.

What, she's alive?

Of course. She first went into hiding in the south, and then she was brought to Cuba. I helped to get her out of the country myself, and she is now in Switzerland. She will get in touch with her parents as soon as she can.

Helga finally located the doctor and took him to task for his many excuses—he had no time; he was too busy; no, tomorrow doesn't work either. Then he was away for a few weeks. And then he denied having said anything about Gisi. He claimed that he did not know her and that Margarita, the nurse, had made everything up. When Helga still did not give up, he said rudely:

Leave me alone, or I will have you committed to the psychiatric ward. You're out of your mind.

Such a harsh response was not unexpected. After all, the women who demanded an explanation of the fate of their children were generally considered crazy by the military regime. Helga did not yield, looked directly into the man's eyes and asked him whether he wasn't ashamed to spread such lies. For a few seconds he was able to match her stare, then, without saying a word, he turned and hurried off.

And since then we have really given up all hope, says Helga, and next to her sits Willi who remains silent.

V
La Paz, Bolivia
1939-1945

The refugees from Europe did not feel at home in Bolivia. It was a poor country with a dozen fabulously wealthy mine owners, two-and-a-half million Indios who were forced to toil on their ancestral lands like slaves, and one-and-a-half million Mestizos who consciously sought to distance themselves from the Indios in their clothing, customs, and reputation. Both groups kept to themselves, either out of necessity or suspicion; they also had no desire to get to know the immigrants more personally. In addition, the immigrants had difficulty communicating in Spanish, and they worked in professions that in La Paz were in little demand. Nevertheless, nearly all of them were eventually able to make a decent living.

Helga's family was an exception. They were not able to escape their precarious financial situation. The Marksteins were industrious and resourceful, and adaptable as well. They were practical in many ways; only in matters of making money were they unsuccessful. At first, they leased a piece of land outside of the city. They planted vegetables, but the harvest was not enough to feed them. Then they tried their luck with a restaurant, *Finca Elma*, which stood on the top of a hill surrounded by nothing but sand and stones, a few anemic eucalyptus trees and dusty cacti.

All of the women in the family, not just Helga's mother, were such excellent cooks that the customers—émigrés from the "Association of Free Austrians" — soon showed up to enjoy the generous portions. The organization celebrated a *Praterfest* there, at which a magician pulled a rabbit from his top-hat, a veiled clairvoyant knew the answer to every question, a farce with the title "The Serial Killer" was performed, everyone sang nostalgic songs of the homeland, and a band played dance music. On Sundays the children helped serve the food, wash the dishes, and stand guard to prevent anyone from bolting from the restaurant before paying the bill. Since the prices they charged barely covered their expenses, they eventually had no choice but to give up the business. Helga's mother then rented a room in the city and helped out in the kitchen of a restaurant on the weekends. Rudolf Markstein got a job as a headwaiter in the first-class Hotel Sucre, and upon his arrival Heinz had an opportunity to learn to become an electrician. Later Heinz worked for a trading company — reluctantly because he was interested in history and literature and he would have preferred to go to college. But there was no money for that. Helga attended an elementary school that the German and Austrian exiles had founded for their children because the public schools were poor and dirty, and the private schools were expensive. She did not learn much; with few exceptions, her teachers had no teaching experience, and most of the students were restless and unruly as a result of their expulsion from Austria. Confusion reigned in the classrooms; basically, the students were left to their own devices.

When she was twelve, Helga began an apprenticeship with a hat-maker. She no longer wanted to be a financial burden on her parents. From her employer, an enormously stingy German immigrant, she only learned how to straighten bent hatpins with a hammer. Once when she accidentally broke a jar, he went on a rampage and swore at her, at which point Helga left the shop for good without saying a word. He later tried to change her mind, but she had already found work elsewhere. In the evening she took a class to learn how to do clerical work—bookkeeping, typing and composing business letters. A girl in the neighborhood who had spent several years in Great Britain taught her the basics of English, which she then improved by reading extensively and by looking up words in the dictionary. She particularly liked the novels of John Steinbeck.

She was already working as a secretary at an import company when the news that World War II was over reached La Paz. Germany had capitulated! Beaming with joy, Helga and all the other employees ran out into the street and hugged each other.

VI
Mendoza, Argentina
1980s

In Mendoza, too, there were women who summoned up the courage to publicly demand information about the where-abouts of their missing loved ones. Like the *Madres de Plaza de Mayo* in Buenos Aires, they met every Thursday in front of the monument to the liberator at the *Plaza San Martín* to voice their concerns. They wore white headscarves and held signs bearing the names and photos of their children. Initially, the security forces beat them, or arrested them, or otherwise sought to disperse them; they were also insulted by passers-by who considered them crazy, but gradually their presence was tolerated. Helga joined them in 1981, four years after Gisi's disappearance and one year before the war for the Islas Malvina,[2] which the military junta began out of an exaggerated sense of their own importance and in anticipation of support from the U.S. government. The junta had counted on its own ability to arouse the patriotic feelings of the Argentineans and hoped to divert attention from the social consequences of the economic crisis. But the ignominious defeat at the hands of the British naval forces accelerated the demise of the dictatorship. Following mass demonstrations and strikes, the last head of the junta,

---

[2] In English, the islands are known as the Falkland Islands.

Reynaldo Bignone, announced democratic elections. In October 1983 the candidate for the Radical Civic Union, Raúl Alfonsín, emerged victorious. During his presidency the commanders-in-chief of the three branches of service were tried and sentenced; the opportunity to pursue further prosecutions was limited by two amnesty laws.

Even before the inauguration of the new president, the political prisoners had been released. These were mainly leftists who had been arrested before the putsch, that is, during the government of Perón's widow, María Estela Martínez. They were mistreated and often received draconian sentences under questionable circumstances from military courts. The conditions in the detention facilities were also terrible, but at least they were not killed, and the government did not deny that they were in the custody of the regime.

Helga and Willi learned from one of those set free, Daniel Ubertone, that the prosecuting attorney, a vice-commodore of the air force, screamed at him during his hearing that he should finally admit that he was distributing flyers, that his denial was futile because they knew all the details of his group's activities, and that they were holding Gisela Tenenbaum, who had long ago confessed.

It is highly probable, actually certain, that the prosecuting attorney was only bluffing. Nevertheless, says Helga, this new information again gave us a reason to be more optimistic.

They imagined that the military had deported the missing to a concentration camp, following the Nazi model, and they expected that the investigative commission that had been empanelled by the Alfonsín government would provide them with some information about their daughter's whereabouts.

We told ourselves that they simply could not have murdered them all. That's just not possible. At least a few hundred must have survived. Where are the secret prisons in which they are held? Their locations should be made public. We'll get them out of there.

Hope faded as more details of the extent of the repression and the treatment of the detainees in the torture centers came to light. Since the lower ranks had already been allowed to plead that they had only followed orders, they did not have to testify in court; the result was that in most cases nothing about the fate of the missing was learned. In addition, the investigative judges did not see any reason to expedite proceedings that involved charges of human rights abuses. Under Alfonsín's successor, Carlos Menem, even the convicted military leaders were pardoned in order to advance the aim of "National Pacification." It was not until June 2005 that the Supreme Court of Argentina declared unconstitutional all those laws that had exempted crimes committed under the dictatorship from punishment. To this day the federal court (number 1) of the province of Mendoza has still not pursued a complaint, filed by the Ecumenical Movement for Human Rights, that alleges the wrongful deprivation of personal liberty, kidnapping, and the murder of fifteen members of the Peron Youth Movement or of the Montoneros, among them Gisela Tenenbaum.

During a trip to Europe in 2003 Helga and Willi read in a Spanish newspaper that, for the first time, a mass grave dating back to the military dictatorship had been found in San Vicente, in the province of Córdoba. Upon their return to Argentina they were directed to the *Equipo Argentino de Antropólogos Forenses* in Buenos Aires, an independent human rights organization that sought to identify the corpses. There they learned that the dead of San Vicente had been hastily buried in 1976, but Helga and Willi nevertheless gave blood samples for DNA testing in case additional corpses were found, and they described their daughter's physical attributes: approximately five feet seven inches, slender with broad shoulders, blue eyes, blond hair, healthy teeth.

And if she were still alive?

For a long time her older sister Heidi was not able to shake the notion that Gisi had lost her identity as a result of having been tortured. That she had become schizophrenic, no longer knew who she was, what her name was, where she came from. That they had simply cast her aside, perhaps sent her abroad. Gisi is alive, but her whereabouts and the kind of life she is living remain unknown — under a different name, without memory, without even knowing that there is such a thing as memory.

VII
Buenos Aires and Mendoza, Argentina
1946-1955

Gisela's parents met in Buenos Aires where Helga had found work as a secretary right after her arrival in November 1946. Heinz Markstein had secretly crossed the border a year earlier; he was able to find a lawyer who helped him (and then his parents and sister) acquire false papers, for a price. According to the new documents, Helga was born in 1929, the daughter of a Czech immigrant, and was entered into the birth registry as Olga.

Heinz introduced her to a group of young people who along with their parents had also been expelled from Vienna and who, from Argentina, had tried to speak out against the injustice of the occupation of Austria. They supported the efforts of the allies in both material and propagandistic ways with fundraisers and aid packages, and they thought about returning to their homeland at the end of the war. But the news about the fate of their relatives who had been in the Nazi extermination camps effected a change of heart in many of them; moreover, they had already grown accustomed to life in Argentina and doubted that they could put down roots in a devastated Europe. Most of them preferred, both here and there, socialist institutions, which they thought, at least at that time, had been realized in the Soviet Union. They had little sympathy for General Juan Domingo Perón, who soon after the military putsch in June 1943 rose to become the most powerful politician in the country and then won the presidential election in February 1946. They saw him as a fascist and a demagogue who wanted to mask the rule of capital through his social and economic reforms. The new proletariat that came into being as a result of the migration to the cities was foreign to them, even if they trusted it to revolutionize society to their liking. It was nationalistic and had no understanding of socialists and communists, or, like its leader, strongly opposed them.

Apart from political and cultural activities, the young Austrians also engaged in sports; in particular, they rowed with the crew team in the Tigre delta on the weekends. Here, on a Sunday in early 1947, Willi and Helga were introduced to each other. Apparently, their mutual interest was limited because they did not see each other for another three years, not until May 1950, when they met at a family gathering. Soon they were a couple—and they would remain a couple. They danced together the whole night, looked deeply into each other's eyes, made a date for the next day, exchanged first kisses on the day after that, and did not hide the fact that they had found their one true love. A month later they were engaged, and on February 10, 1951 they were married.

Since 1938, Willi had been living with his mother, Laura, in Buenos Aires, at first in a *conventillo*, a tenement house with little sunlight, in the Palermo district. He had grown up without a father in Ottakring, in an apartment building near the *Brunnenmarkt*; his talent, dubious to be sure, was his ability to erase painful experiences from his memory, along with their locations, so that he recalled very little of his youth in Vienna and his journey to Argentina. In Vienna he had begun to work for a jeweler while attending a technical school in the evening. With his diploma he easily found a position as a construction technician. The young married couple dreamed of a small house and garden in one of the suburbs and acquired a parcel of land in Caseros, near the Pacífico rail line. But then Willi ran into an old friend whom he had not seen in a long time. The man, a chemist by profession, was now living in Mendoza; he was enthusiastic about the tranquility of everyday life in this provincial city at the foot of the Andes, about its natural beauty, and about the agreeable climate. He told Willi that he intended to open up a laboratory because he had developed a new cooling medium for refrigerators. He claimed one could earn a fortune with his invention. If Willi and his young wife would like to join him, the three of them together could share the start-up costs. In addition, he said he needed reliable and educated partners for the management team and for the distribution of the product. Willi was all for it even if he did not understand anything about it. He had always wanted to live in a rural environment, far away from the hustle and bustle of the big city. And Helga was accustomed to changing residences every few years. So they were mindful of their expenses, limited them to a minimum, sold their parcel of land, and sent money to Mendoza each month. The man wrote back that the business was coming along, and that, for the time being, they should not jump the gun but remain in the capital. He would tell them in good time when they should come to Mendoza. But a year later, they were no longer willing to remain in Buenos Aires. They quit their jobs, packed their belongings, and sold what they thought they could do without, before boarding a train on November

2, 1952. The next day they arrived in Mendoza. The sun was shining, not a single cloud in the sky, and in the west the snow-capped Andes soared majestically, incredibly.

Although they had sent him a telegram announcing the time of their arrival, they had to ring their partner's doorbell to awaken him. Embarrassed but without beating around the bush, he admitted that he had lied to them from the very beginning and that he had neither developed a new cooling agent nor rented a laboratory. He said that he did not even pursue a regular job but lived off of gullible people like themselves whom he could fleece with his empty promises. He then gambled away the money in the city's casino. Helga and Willi refrained from filing a complaint. Their savings were gone; what good would it do to put their partner behind bars. Since they now found themselves in Mendoza, which they liked, they decided to try to make their fortune there. They found a cheap room, and lived on tomatoes, bread, and grapes. They trudged around to the grocery stores and coffee houses as sales representatives for a new kind of cocoa powder. A few weeks later Helga found out in a routine exam that she was three months pregnant. While she was happy, Willi was rather worried. They had hardly managed to survive on their own as two people, how could they make it as three? Besides that, they had no experience with children. Helga had been the youngest in her family, and Willi could not remember ever having held a baby. Gradually his concern about how they would survive proved unfounded; when the owner of a drugstore needed a reliable employee, she hired Willi. She also told them that after their baby was born they could stay in two rooms in the back wing of her residence, a former mansion, without bath or shower but with a large inner courtyard and a beautiful wine arbor.

On June 15, 1953, Helga gave birth to a healthy girl. She named her Heidi after the heroine of a novel by the Swiss author Johanna Spyri, which she had read when she was ten. In spite of Willi's fears, they quite naturally learned how to care for the baby, and when they were unsure what to do they followed the advice in Dr. Spock's *Baby and Child Care*, a modern handbook for parents published in the United States that Helga's cousin Trixi had sent as a gift. Heidi was a cheerful and trusting child. She slept through the night and only rarely cried, so that soon Helga felt like doing something new. Circumstances had forced her to work from a very early age; she now wanted to study something that would be useful to others, such as medicine. Willi encouraged her in her decision. But to be admitted to the university, Helga first had to complete the final year of required schooling. She finished it in a month along with some eleven- and twelve-year-old girls. When she stepped into the school courtyard after completing her final exam, she could see not only the parents of the other children but also Willi, standing behind the baby carriage that held Heidi. Helga's enthusiasm rubbed off on him, and he too decided to study medicine. Together they registered for courses at the secondary level. In December 1954 they took the exams covering the first year's material. Five weeks later, on February 4, 1955, Gisi was born.

VIII
Mendoza, Argentina
1953-1976

First there was the hope. The pain, too, was there, from the very beginning. The hope faded, the pain became entrenched. And then a new feeling arose. It expressed itself covertly. For a long time it could not be defined. Was it frustration or exhaustion, or the inability to accept what had happened? Yes, all of these, but something more. Anger or rather rage, *bronca*, a word in which hatred resonates, but also powerlessness and humiliation, and the certainty that Gisi's efforts had been in vain. A few days ago one of Gisi's friends had said something to her, Heidi, that broke her heart: *Lo que más me duele de tu hermana: que se pensó todo esto al pedo.* Your sister took everything so seriously. To the very end, she believed in it all. In the people, in the revolution, in better times. Anger —because Gisi had voluntarily exposed herself to danger, because she had overestimated her strength, because she was too proud to get out at the right time, because she refused to accept others' help, because she was convinced that she was doing the right thing. But the so-called "people" did not want to have anything to do with her goals. The people were not as bad off as they are today. They wanted to be left in peace. They supported those who promised them a line of credit for a house, a raise, a television, and a used car. They also supported those who maintained order so that the businessmen could pursue their deals without interference. Stop the demon- strations, stop the strikes, stop the assassinations and the kidnappings. Television instead of revolts. Soccer until they go gaga.

Bronca just because of Gisi's stubbornness, because of her lack of insight, because of her confidence, because of the fact that her disappearance has transformed all their lives and she had not taken that into consideration. Nothing is like it was. New Year's Eve, birthdays, wedding anniversaries, any distinction like the *medalla de honor,* any special occasion to celebrate together with the whole family — someone is always missing, the joy is always muted. One could get beyond a premature death if the loved one died in an accident or of a serious illness. One would also find a way, in time, to deal with the loss of Gisi if she were the victim of a common crime or if her death resulted from some kind of wrongful act. Of course, she was murdered. It would be absurd to doubt that. But her body, or whatever remains of her, has not been recovered. How does one mourn a sister, a daughter, an aunt, a great aunt who is both absent and present? No one in the family knows how to deal with this situation; everyone responds differently.

Heidi noticed, for example, that she often confused Gisi with her youngest sister, Mónica, a self-protective mechanism, what else? For a long time, they appeared as one person in her dreams, as if she had had only one sister. As long as Heidi is awake, Gisi is present to her, unique, unmistakable, pure. But in her subconscious mind Gisi's image has faded, she has fused with Mónica, so that she, Heidi, is constantly forced to ask herself: Did Gisela Tenenbaum, my sister, ever really exist? Is what I remember true? Who is that eight-year-old girl with the blond curls that I see in front of me, in the playpen that our parents actually purchased for me because I could quickly get away when they were momentarily occupied with something else. I'm now sitting in front of it, just two-and-half years old, outdoors on the ground, on the outside of the wooden slats through which I reach for the toy duck, for the building blocks, for the doll, to take them from her, very slowly, piece by piece, and she sits across from me, on the other side, with *bronca*, and can't stop me.

This scene, this image is her earliest memory of Gisi.

Her last memory goes back to the year 1976 when Paola, Heidi's oldest daughter, was three months old. Paola was born in May, on the nineteenth, so it must have been in winter, in mid-August. Heidi and Oscar, her husband Oscar Mussuto, were living at that time in the barrio Cano, in the apartment that Helga's mother had left them. Oscar was not at home — Gisi knew it, otherwise she would not have come, because he would have shown her the door. She was hardly recognizable since she had dyed her hair black and wore it short. It was the first and only time that she saw her little niece, and she brought her a gift, a red teddy bear that Paola still has today. She referred to Paola by her other name, Verónica.

Heidi's daughter actually had two names: Verónica and Paola. After the child's birth Heidi had insisted on calling Paola, Verónica, and Oscar insisted that Verónica be called Paola. Neither wanted to give in, because Heidi found the name Paola horrible, and for Oscar, Verónica was terrible. Consequently, they argued, fiercely, they argued a lot anyway, all the time to tell the truth, and so they argued over the child's name. It began with the fact that Heidi had desperately wanted a boy, and they had agreed that if the baby were in fact a boy, she would choose the name, and if it were a girl, then Oscar would get to choose. Heidi was absolutely convinced that it would be a boy, but it was a girl, which caused a blow-up, because Oscar wanted to call her Ariadna Paola, which Heidi found particularly hideous, and so she said she should be able to give the child at least one of the names. For two weeks her daughter lived without a name. Then Oscar finally accepted Verónica, but insisted on calling her Paola, which she still opposed. Neither of them gave in. Gisi knew nothing of this argument because in the letters that Heidi wrote her she always spoke only of Verónica, which is why she always called her niece Verónica, Vera, Verita. This is how matters stood when Heidi saw Gisi for the final time, but the dispute between Heidi and Oscar about the name went on for yet another year. He: Paola. She: Verónica.

Until finally Mónica, her other sister, said to Heidi: look, you are the mother, be reasonable, give in, think of the child, she might even be harmed by this quarrelling. Mónica had just read a book about a woman named Sybil who had suffered from multiple personality disorder in part because her father gave her one name and her mother another. That really happened, said Mónica, so give in, for the sake of your daughter's health, call her Paola. Her own father liked Paola better anyway, but one of Oscar's brothers was on her side. Okay. Paola won out, a name that Heidi dislikes even today, and now she no longer knows how she got on the topic, oh right, because Gisi called Paola Verónica. Because whenever she wrote Gisi a few lines, Heidi never mentioned Paola, always only Verónica.

No idea why Gisi asked her for a comb, presumably to comb her hair, what else for, at any rate the memory of the comb has stayed with her. Gisi absent-mindedly put it in her pocket; she had arrived some time in the morning and stayed two-and-a-half or three hours. Heidi thinks that they even ate lunch together, and then Gisi left. From the balcony Heidi follows her with her eyes, observes her sister cross the lawn in front of the house (the apartment was located on the second floor, a nice apartment, the whole complex was nice; there was even a children's playground with a sandbox and a swing on the lawn.) She wants to call out, the comb, you forgot to give me back the comb. But then Heidi thinks, she can keep the comb, it doesn't matter.

Not for a second did it occur to me that I had seen my sister for the last time.

IX
Mendoza, Argentina
1955-1960

Heidi still finds it incomprehensible today that those who passed her on the street, even friends of the family, confused her with Gisi or that total strangers bent down over them to admire the assumed twins close up when Helga or Willi took them for a walk, for example, in San Martín Park. For, apart from the fact that their parents dressed them the same, either because that was more convenient or because it was customary to do so, the two sisters differed from each other from an early age—in the color of their hair and eyes and in their temperament. Heidi was lively, sociable, and sometimes misbehaved; Gisi was quiet and observant, and had a strong will. Whenever Helga asked her older daughter to bring her something, for example, some silk thread or a spice, Heidi grumbled, I can't, but Gisi immediately jumped up *yo sí puedo*! and pushed a chair to the cabinet or the kitchen cupboard, climbed up and brought back the desired object. Or when they were planning to do something, an excursion into the mountains or a walk over a narrow bridge or perhaps they simply were supposed to take the trash out to the street, and their parents asked, who's going first, who's going to help, Gisi exclaimed: *Yo la primera!*

Yo soy la segunda, Heidi said. It didn't matter much to her that she was second in these things. Her sister's ambition never bothered her; at least she, Heidi, was not constantly the center of attention.

In the initial weeks after the birth of her sister, it did indeed bother her that her parents were no longer solely concerned with her. She felt particularly neglected whenever Gisi was nursed. It was on just such occasions that she wanted her mother to pick her up, and if her complaining did not help, then she would climb up onto her mother, onto her lap, and from her lap to her shoulder, from where she attempted to sit on Helga's head. To fend off such disruptions, Helga resorted to a method that was not in Dr. Spock's handbook for young parents: with Gisi in her arms, she climbed up onto the table, pulled a chair up behind her, sat down as if on a throne, and opened her blouse to allow Gisi to nurse. Heidi used the opportunity to slip quietly into the bedroom where she emptied a jar of ink on the bedspread, or she went into the kitchen where she attacked a saucepan of cocoa, or she went into the courtyard where someone had forgotten to remove the ladder leaning against the roof. When Helga got around to checking on her, she was already standing on the top rung.

    The apartment was located in Calle Buenos Aires, in the middle of the city, where there were numerous businesses and shops but only a few apartment buildings. That had the disadvantage that there were not many neighbors who could look after the children when Helga had to run an errand. Willi was indispensable at the drugstore, as store manager, accountant, clerk, sales person, and cashier. So Helga usually took her daughters with her when she went out. But one day she had no choice but to leave the children alone for half an hour. When she returned, they were hardly recognizable in the drifts of feathers; in her absence Heidi had inspected the inner life of a down comforter.

When Gisi turned two, Helga placed the girls in the daycare center at the *Centro Cultural Israelita*. Heidi felt at home there from the very first day and immediately made friends with the other children. Gisi, on the other hand, did not have a playmate and sat crying in the corner the whole time, according to Heidi. Helga was undecided whether she should take her younger daughter out of the center. Every morning she asked her, would you rather stay with me? No, said Gisi and shook her head emphatically. And I will definitely not cry any more.

The *Centro Cultural Israelita* was not an elitist club. It encouraged members who, like Willi and Helga, had to carefully watch their expenses. In spite of its name, the center did not discriminate with respect to religion or cultural difference, and it regularly invited scientists, intellectuals and artists to give lectures. The singer Victor Heredia, who much later became famous for a song about his missing sister, gave one of his first concerts there. For Willi, it was the place where he could meet people who shared his passion for politics; and it was also a good substitute for the "Movement for a Free Austria" in Buenos Aires. He was among the first of his friends there to become disillusioned with the kind of socialism practiced in the Soviet Union. But it was still the Communists with whom he got along best. He discussed issues with them, bought their party newspaper, *Nuestra Palabra*, and respected most of them for their personal integrity even if he reproached them for their blind allegiance to Moscow's party line and their flawed understanding of Argentine reality; in private, he also criticized their attitude toward the indigenous lower classes. It was not that they considered themselves better, but they had, both professionally and privately, little contact to the *cabecitas negras*, the little black heads, as the poor in the rural areas are still called today either pejoratively or naively. He was somewhat disappointed that his daughters were not at all interested in politics when they grew a bit older, while the children of his friends in the Club knew an astounding amount about the Great Socialist October Revolution, the Battle at Stalingrad, the Korean War, and the inherent contradictions of the Argentine bourgeoisie.

Helga and Willi completed the required five years of schooling with unfailing enthusiasm and discipline. In the first four years they did not have to attend the evening classes; it sufficed that they showed up for the final exams. But they were required to take the final year's classes, so in the late afternoons they left home together. A female friend looked after the children until they returned. Perhaps it was then, or probably one or two years later, that Heidi began to be afraid of the dark when her parents were not home. Willi and Helga had purchased a bunk bed for their daughters; when the older daughter, Heidi, who slept on the top bunk, stretched out her arm to her sister below, Gisi would grasp it and night after night tell her a story to calm her fears. Heidi no longer recalls the details, but it had to do with robbers or monsters who were after her and who gave her the creeps. But she knew that Gisi's story always had a happy ending, and so in the last second Gisi would come riding in on a splendid white horse and rescue her from the clutches of the villains.

This *idée fixe* to save others. The Redeemer Syndrome, even then, says Heidi.

She no longer knows how long her sister held her hand before she fell asleep. Presumably, she gently loosened her hold, placed Heidi's arm back up on her bed, and arranged her pillow before she fell asleep herself.

In November 1958 Helga and Willi completed their required schooling, each receiving a 10, the highest grade, and they began to study for the medical school's entrance examination. Eight hundred students applied for one hundred and twenty seats. As they nervously checked the results of the exam, they saw their names among those who had passed, Guillermo Tenenbaum was twelfth and Olga Markstein de Tenenbaum was fortieth. Following the summer vacation, in March, as Heidi entered first grade, her parents began to attend the lectures. Willi spent the mornings at the university, and Helga took courses in the afternoon. She pored over her books (in the first year, anatomy, chemistry and physics) until Willi got up at three o'clock and took his turn. He had had to give up the job in the drugstore; the owner was not willing to keep him at a reduced workload. Two friends helped him get a job selling laboratory supplies.

More lucrative and more permanent, however, was another activity: a crabby nurse at the *Hospital Central* showed Helga and Willi how to give injections and what to pay attention to while giving them. The woman considered it unreasonable to have to teach this skill to students who had only just begun their studies a few weeks earlier. Nevertheless, the family was able to live, however modestly, from giving the shots. But it did create a rather rigid daily routine for them. At that time penicillin had to be administered every four hours, which meant that Willi was rarely able to sleep through the night.

Toward the end of the first year at the university Helga became pregnant for the third time. They soon had to look for a new apartment; the owner of the house terminated the lease because it had come to his attention that Guillermo Tenenbaum was a communist, and he preferred not to have such people under his roof especially since the federal police were located just a few doors down the street. At the *Centro Cultural Israelita* Willi and Helga had made friends with a couple who owned a pharmacy in Las Heras. From them they learned that an apartment just across the way in the Calle Lisandro Moyano was to become vacant in a few months. Two bedrooms, a living room, kitchen and bath; the rent was affordable. Shortly after the move, on July 29, 1960, Mónica was born. It was Helga's thirtieth birthday.

Because money was tight, but perhaps also because it seemed natural for those who had grown up in Red Vienna, Willi and Helga made use of the communal facilities of the city. If there was no cost to use the outdoor communal pool, why should they go to the effort to join a private club, with whose members they would have little in common anyway? Heidi and Gisi learned how to swim at a summer camp run by the *Centro Cultural Israelita*; Gisi was two or three years old. One day she drew the attention of a swimming instructor from the *gimnasio municipal*; he encouraged her parents to nurture her talent. At a public swimming exhibition, the youth trainer of YPF, the swim club of the national oil company, threw Gisi into the water with her hands and legs bound together. After she surfaced, she swam several lengths seemingly effortlessly. When she got rid of the cords and climbed out of the pool at the end of the performance, the trainer walked over to her and asked her name.

Gisela Tenenbaum, she said.

A fine name for a swimming champion, he replied.

He got her into the club, and Gisi finished second in her first race, without having completed a single hour of training. Heidi and later Mónica were also accepted onto the YPF swim team. They did not have to pay the membership fee, which her parents would hardly have been able to afford anyway. Just the bus fare to Godoy Cruz, where the club's pool was located, put a strain on the family budget.

X
Mendoza, Argentina
1960–1983

Kuki Giménez was eight when the Tenenbaum family moved into the neighborhood, which at that time was rather run-down. According to Kuki, the houses looked rather shabby, as if they were still unfinished. The streets were unpaved, and depending on the weather the busses and trucks either stirred up clouds of dust behind them or rumbled through knee-deep puddles. There was a soccer field, but it consisted mainly of bare, trampled dirt with a few blades of grass on the sidelines. It was not advisable to invite friends home, which is what Kuki found out, because his parents were strict, *jodidos*, as he says, impatient. Indeed they had violent tempers. The noise of running and shouting children enraged them; and he would be beaten if he brought home poor grades, talked back to them or showed up with torn pants because he got into a fight with the older boys.

Kuki only noticed that there was another kind of parenting when he became friends with Heidi and Gisi. And he was not alone; his classmates Quito and Hugo observed it as well. Hugo's father was a soldier by profession but at least he did not scold his children all the time; he was one of the first on the block to own a television, and the children all sat in front of it, punctually at 5:30 PM, so that they would not miss the crazy adventures of Captain Piluso and his friend Coquito. After the show they ran back to the Tenenbaum's apartment to play because they got a glass of milk there. Every child who wants to succeed in his adventures has to drink a glass of milk every day; that is what Piluso and Coquito asserted, and Guillermo and Helga confirmed this. Only Gisi showed concern when they remarked that many parents do not have the money to buy milk for their children.

It's not the case that Gisi's parents were too lenient, not at all, but, Kuki says, they did give him the feeling that he was always welcome. Unlike many adults, they did not tolerate their children's outrageous behavior. The two were simply extraordinary, beloved in the whole neighborhood, although they did not aim to be popular. They were helpful, of course, and they were unpretentious; they did not consider themselves better than anyone else although they no doubt were. They lived modestly, and they willingly accepted the burden of spending additional semesters at the university; they were not motivated by the prospect of winning the lottery. When Kuki first met Helga and Willi, they were still biking to their patients because they did not have money for the bus. But they did send their daughters to the swim club. Kuki claims that it would never have occurred to his parents to pay for him to become a member of a sports club.

He got along especially well with Heidi. She was more high-spirited than her sister, adventurous. She was always game for a prank: to ring someone's doorbell and then run away. Or throw water balloons from the balcony. Or sneak into courtyards and smear shoe polish on the freshly hung laundry. Gisi rarely went along, not out of cowardice, but because she felt sorry for the neighbors who were the victims of their pranks. She preferred to stay home and study or read, even later when the others would go dancing on

Saturday evenings or Sunday afternoons. There were no discotheques, so they met in private houses, if possible when the parents were not home. Everyone brought something: Coca-Cola, empanadas, sandwiches with mortadella. Or they made arrangements for a picnic. Or they went to the movies. There was no other form of entertainment, as far as they knew.

Gisi was a superb swimmer. When she participated in a championship meet, everybody went to the club to cheer her on. Heidi also swam competitively. But Gisi was better. For a while Heidi was Kuki's girlfriend. Holding hands, making out a little, nothing more was imaginable at the time. But then they got into an argument, his fault because he had cheated on her. He was all about *joda*, partying, and didn't take fidelity too seriously; one day Heidi had a new boyfriend. But even before that she and Kuki had had a big falling out, and then Kuki's family found a new apartment; the Tenenbaums moved a block away, to the Calle Juan Jufré, and gradually they lost contact with one another. Occasionally, he ran into Gisi at the technical college, but only rarely because he was taking evening courses as he completed his military duty, and her lectures were in the afternoon.

In 1976, he began working as a civilian airplane technician for the air force. He was two years ahead of Gisi at college. He did not know that she was politically active. He was never interested in politics himself, and she never attempted to talk to him about it, probably because she was aware of his work with the military. Only after the fact did Kuki learn from Guillermo and Helga that Gisi had disappeared. Although he serviced military planes in the fourth brigade the whole time, he never noticed anything unusual. Sometimes they, the civilians, would be sent home early. Clearly no unsolicited witnesses were wanted. But he never gave it a second thought. Today it is said that members of his brigade tortured and murdered opponents of the regime in a shed near the airport in Las Lajas. He knew nothing of this.

By and large, things were quiet in Mendoza. And when something did happen, there was silence. This is how they are, the *mendocinos*, says Kuki: careful and tight-lipped. Even after the military rule ended, there were no massive demonstrations. Only the *Madres* demonstrated at the *Plaza San Martín*. Once, when he went by, he saw them there. But he did not join the protest, nor did Quito, nor Hugo who had not lived in Las Heras for some time but had moved with his parents to the countryside. It would not have been advisable to be seen on the square, especially for someone like him, who owed his modest livelihood to the military. Moreover, as I said before, Kuki was never interested in politics. It is rather odd that he now finds himself engaged in politics. The civilian employees of the armed forces have been unionized since 1983, and he is now one of the union representatives.

Does this ultimately have anything to do with Gisi?

XI
Storozhynets, Romania
1934

Helga too had learned to swim at an early age.

In the summer of 1934 Fanny Markstein took the children to Bukovina to visit her relatives in the small town of Storozhynets.[3] Her parents had separated when she was sixteen; while her mother moved to Vienna with the four younger children, her father and her oldest sister had stayed behind in Storozhynets. And now Fanny yearned for a reunion; she wanted to show Heinz and Helga the region where she had grown up. It was Helga's first trip by train, and it seemed nearly endless to the four-year-old—a day and a half through the flat lands and the valleys of the Carpathian Mountains, past the cornfields, meadows, orchards, and swamps. She kneeled on the seat, pressed her nose against the windowpane, and marveled that the world was so large and strange.

Helga had heard nothing good about her grandfather. As a metalworker he was highly regarded; he knew his craft and had achieved some prosperity. But he was very strict with his children and put them to work at an early age. He was also extremely stingy, which his own family felt most directly. At twelve, Fanny possessed only one pair of shoes,

---

[3] At the time Storozhynets was part of Romania. It currently lies in Ukraine.

which she had long since worn out, but it was not easy to make her father see that she desperately needed a new pair. When he finally ordered them from the small-town shoemaker, he insisted that they be made four sizes larger, 38 instead of 34, since his daughter was still growing, and it was out of the question to have her measured for new shoes again in a year or two.

And the dumb thing was that my feet stopped growing at size 36, said Helga's mother. But that did not bother your grandpa.

Now, however, there was no sign of his thrift. Whenever his granddaughter from Vienna visited him in his stately house on Market Square—and that happened almost every morning during their stay in Storozhynets—he slipped her a coin so that she could buy some ice cream. He lived with a young woman and bred canaries, which Helga always admired. As much as Helga liked visiting her grandfather, she was even happier to visit Aunt Lotte, who lived with her husband and two teenage children, Hilde and Erwin, in a modest wooden house at the edge of town (the oldest daughter, Grete, attended the secondary school in Czernowitz). She was a cheerful person, happy to have unexpected guests. Helga wandered through the beech forests in the surrounding area with her uncle; he told her of the frightfully howling wolves who prowled around the houses on bitterly cold winter nights, and she was overcome by a warming thrill as she reached for his hand, the feeling of happiness, the feeling of security in the face of constant peril.

This feeling did not leave her even when she almost drowned in the Seret River, which is about a half-hour walk from town. One morning Heinz wanted to go to the river to swim with Hilde and Erwin. Helga passionately pleaded with her mother, who finally gave in and let her go with them. Aunt Lotte was able to allay her mother's fears saying that her children were responsible, they would certainly watch out for her. But then at a rather desolate spot along the Seret River, Hilde and Erwin decided to swim to the opposite bank. They challenged Heinz to join them. He did not feel good about leaving his sister alone, but he also did not want to be thought a coward by the older children. So he told Helga, emphatically, that she was not to move from where she was standing, that they would be right back. Helga nodded, gazed after them, and went about building a mud castle with a moat around it. As she scooped water from the river, she took one step forward, then another, then a third, until suddenly the ground went out from under her.

His guilty conscience made Heinz look back at her every few seconds. He had already reached the middle of the river when he no longer could see her; he gave a shout and turned back. Today Helga says that he must have flown, but in fact he really did swim. In any case she was still conscious when he pulled her from the water; he held her upside down and shook her. Helga coughed pathetically, and a ton of water flowed out of her mouth. Then she began to thrash about and wanted to be set down on the ground again. In contrast to the others, she wasn't terribly upset.

That was close, said Heinz, who was trembling. We better not mention this to Mama; that would needlessly upset her.

Okay, said Helga.

In fact, they remained quiet about the incident both

during the visit with their aunt and on the trip home three weeks later. They were accompanied by their grandfather's going-away present, two caged canaries, which they called Pupsi and Pipsi.

Not until they had been back in Vienna for a while did Heinz dare to confess to his parents that Helga had almost drowned in the Seret. But before he did, that very summer, he taught her how to swim in the old Danube.

XII
Mendoza, Argentina
1960s

It is possible that twenty-nine years later Helga still recalls the hot day in February 1963 when the Tenenbaums took a similarly long train ride to Tarija, Bolivia, where they were to be met by Helga's other aunts. It is also possible that this was the first time that she and Willi spoke with their two older daughters about the family members who had died. Only two of their cousins in Storozhynets, Hilde and Grete, survived the crimes of the Nazis.

In the San Juan desert, the middle of nowhere, the train jumped the rails. Apart from a few bruises and scrapes the passengers were not hurt; the Tenenbaum family escaped with only a scare. At the behest of the train crew, all of the passengers climbed down from the rail cars and placed their luggage on the embankment. The men reviewed the damage and, having become talkative because of the scare, outdid each other in describing accidents that they had either experienced themselves or been witness to, pointing out that some of those involved had survived without harm or while others perished. In the meantime, the women fished out their travel provisions, and the children complained that they were thirsty or urgently had to go to the bathroom.

There was sand everywhere, but no rocks large enough to provide them with some shade. Willi built a wall out of their suitcases and bags so that at least little Mónica could be more or less protected from the blazing sun and the gusts of wind.

It was already growing dark when a replacement train of only three cars arrived from the opposite direction. In the bustling of the moment they lost sight of Gisi. Even Heidi did not know where her sister was. While Willi took care of the luggage, both Helga, with Mónica in her arms, and Heidi ran about nervously, fought their way through the crowd of people looking to grab a seat, and called out for Gisi. In vain. Helga reconciled herself to the fact that the train might depart without her. Then they finally saw her leaning out of a car window and waving with all her might: Come here, quick, I have seats for us all.

That was typical of her, says Helga. Always very *responsable*. She did the right thing of her own accord. No one ever had to tell her what to do.

The same at school. From the very beginning Gisi's diligence, humility, and compassion, not to mention her distinctive penmanship, had set her apart. In November 1962 her teacher wrote on her report card: *Tienes sentimientos muy elevados y gran inteligencia, Gisela.* You have sublime feelings and great intelligence. Nurture them! But in her seventh and final year at elementary school, Gisi was not named *abanderada* (the student chosen to raise the Argentine flag on national holidays, for example, on Flag Day or on the anniversary of the May Revolution, the Declaration of Independence, or the death of General San Martín). She was only second, *escolta*, which had to do with the fact that her father was a very principled man, according to Heidi. Willi was of the opinion that children have to manage their homework on their own; in Austria, he said, when I was in elementary school, my mother did not help me—all you have to do is pay attention in class. If his children had not understood something, then of course they could consult him. But unlike other parents, Helga and Willi insisted that their daughters be responsible for their own homework. They created favorable conditions for studying, attempted to maintain a household routine, and in general did a lot with their children. They had confidence in them, and this confidence included the ability to solve their own problems.

Heidi also had talent. But she did not take her homework seriously; she wanted to be with her friends as soon as she could. It sometimes amazed her father that she apparently did not have to study for a particular class whereas Gisi, two grades behind her, spent whole afternoons studying for the same class. Gisi always brought home the best grades, an eight, a nine, and even a ten, while Heidi's grades were all over the place. To preclude any trouble, Heidi decided to hide her monthly report cards, which Willi and Helga had to sign as parents, among those of her sister. It was a thick pile, with Gisi's good grades on top, and she hoped that her father would be so tired in the evening from his work and his internship that he would just sign them and not pay any attention to the grades. It didn't work. The result was a good scolding, as there were often such scoldings, at least that is how the youngest sister remembers it: all five of us at the table, Heidi blubbering, with tears in her eyes, Willi with raised voice reading her the riot act, Gisi, calm and composed, making her point without any fear of her father.

She protected me from him, says Heidi. Because when worse came to worst, we naturally closed ranks. That probably had to do with the fact that we were so different. We had different interests, different goals, and different ideas about what is important in life. That's why we were seldom at odds with one another. Of course, we got into arguments, that is normal among siblings; even then I talked a lot, *la boc-chut, boc-chut* Gisi shouted whenever my chattering got on her nerves, that is, I should keep my mouth shut. Or, in order to upset me, she would call me *pelirroja*. That was a sore point with me. Under no circumstances did I want to acknowledge that I had red hair. I jumped up, and blind with rage chased her from one room to the next, out onto the balcony and back inside again, around the kitchen table, across our parents' bed, and when I caught her, I pulled her hair. Still, for the most part, we got along well with each other.

But even the little bit of fighting got my father's goat. He accepted arguing about important topics – politics, society, and history. At home, however, there was supposed to be harmony. I never really experienced my parents arguing with each other. That later became a problem for me and for Mónica in our marriages; we assessed our marriages in light of our parents' and found ours to be wanting. It took a while for us to see that our marital crises were the norm and that their harmonious marriage represented the exception.

Gisi turned out like her father. Willi's friends also noticed this, and they occasionally teased him that his second-born could be mistaken for him. But you couldn't tell by looking at the two of them that they were even related; Gisi had Helga's eyes and hair while Heidi and Mónica, with their slender limbs and chestnut-brown eyes, looked more like their father. But Gisi's temperament, her character! Gisela is Guillermo's son, his friends said, and meant that she had developed all the virtues that generally speaking were judged masculine. She was circumspect, disciplined, and earnest. In addition, she was not out to please people. Everything that was superficial was frowned upon in the Tenenbaum household, and Gisi accepted that, not out of obedience but rather because deep inside she believed it to be right. She read books and newspapers, collected stamps, and listened to the news on foreign radio stations, while Heidi was already trying out different hairstyles in front of the mirror and painting her fingernails.

I had a terrible time with my father; painted fingernails were a bourgeois anathema to him.

Heidi was not interested in politics, neither then nor later. Whenever Helga and Willi attended lectures in the *Centro Cultural Israelita* with their daughters, Gisi listened attentively while Heidi just sat there, bored, and thought about something else.

Seen in this light, says Heidi, Gisi really was her father's child. But that is not to say that he showed any special preference for her. With respect to his children, he treated us all the same. By no means did he indoctrinate her, nor did he brainwash her. They simply had common interests. I could have shared them; it was an offer I refused. I was not less loved for my choice. And my mother, who is very savvy, emphasized my father's good qualities: his magnanimity, his intelligence, and his willingness to help others. She was a companion much like those in storybooks. She kept us together; she kept our passions in check; she was the moderating force in our family. She operated more in the background. She later told me that she often had to secretly laugh at my pranks. I had never noticed that.

It never occurred to her to contradict my father when he scolded me. Maybe it was right that way. There were never two fronts at home. It was always clear what was right and what was wrong. My sister internalized this way of thinking. Even with respect to swimming. Gisi did not win championship after championship because she was in particularly great shape physically, but because of her character. She had a well-defined sense of responsibility, and she adhered to a training regimen that was, to her mind, appropriate. If she had to swim, then she just swam; if she had to train for twenty-four hours, then she would just train for twenty-four hours. It never would have occurred to her to object. I, too, did not complain, but I didn't like it; for me it was an irksome duty that my father insisted on. But to be honest, it did not matter to me whether I could keep up with the competition, whether I was last or nearly drowned in the middle of the race. Gisi was intent on beating her own best time, and I checked out the boys to see if there was one whom I liked. Not yet in those days, but soon.

XIII
Mendoza, Argentina
1960s–1970s

First, there was the business with the bathing cap, and then her behavior at the junior championship meet. Two anecdotes that clearly demonstrate Gisi's character—to the extent that that is even necessary.

The twin sisters Cristina and Ana María Ferrer were twelve, four years older than Gisi, when they joined the swim team at YPF. They had a scholarship and trained for free since their parents would also never have been able to come up with the money for a membership. On the very first day they befriended Gisi. It was impossible not to be fond of her because she was selfless, ready to help, strong-willed, and had no discernible need to get the better of the other swimmers. At the same time, brilliant, in every respect. At a certain age, of course, almost everyone wants to be in the limelight. But not Gisi. She won championships, but winning seemed almost to embarrass her. Her face turned beet red when her name appeared on the display board or when there was a photo of her in the newspaper.

Now the story of the bathing cap, and what happened at the awards ceremony following the juniors meet. But before that, Cristina and Ana María want to make clear that they considered Gisi much more than a friend. She was a sister to them, more than a sister. A special being, an angel. That is how she looked, with her freckles and blond, stubborn curls, which she had braided into pigtails, and how she acted, like an angel—as when she quickly filled in for Cristina in the juniors or when one of the girls forgot her bathing cap. In any case, the three were soon inseparable. Cristina and Ana María were frequently at her house; they often played together, ate lunch or dinner together, or listened to music together. The difference in their ages did not matter. Cristina and Ana María's parents were just as enthusiastic about Gisi as their daughters were. They adored her, virtually venerated her. And vice versa, Gisi's parents accepted Cristina and Ana María as part of their family. Gisi was also beloved at the club. Even by the few girls who wanted to excel at any cost and who saw Gisi as their competition. There were always girls who left their bathing caps at home, and without a cap they were not allowed to get in the pool. More than once, Gisi tore the cap off her head right after touching the wall to toss it to another girl. That was the first thing she thought of. And only then did she ask about her time.

Gisi stopped swimming at fifteen. Now she wanted to learn German, she said. Besides, she had an allergic reaction to chlorine; her complaints about her sinuses had become more frequent over the years. Cristina and Ana María continued for another year, and then they too stopped swimming competitively. They no longer had much contact with Gisi, but they did not lose sight of each other all together, and if they had not seen each other for two weeks, then the three friends would talk on the phone. Cristina and Ana María were university students by then, studying journalism and physical education, respectively. In 1976, before the final exams, Ana María went to Spain. In Denia she managed to earn a living as a swimming instructor, and then she worked for a few years in Italy. Cristina completed her studies in Mendoza, but instead of applying for a job as a journalist, she took a position as an elementary school teacher.

The political situation had already begun to heat up. Even in Mendoza people hit the streets. It began in April 1972 when the teachers demonstrated for better pay. Other professional groups soon joined them. But instead of dealing with their demands, the government of General Alejandro Lanusse increased the cost of electricity. This resulted in rioting, looting, and street fighting between the demonstrators and the police. A state of emergency was declared in the whole province. Lanusse finally felt compelled to retract the price hikes and to increase wages. For one week at least, Mendoza was in the vanguard of the resistance to the authority of the state and to the cuts in social services. By that time Cristina and Ana María had hidden at least a dozen young people at their house for a few days and nights because of the curfew and also because military troops were constantly patrolling the streets. Their mother made a stew in a large, old, blackened kettle that had not been used in years. Distressed, their father withdrew to his bedroom but did not raise any objection to the invasion of the uninvited guests although he found the demonstrations unnecessary; and he would have lost his job as an official in the public printing company if the authorities had searched his house. But the repression following the *Mendozazo* was child's play compared with what happened after the putsch, when assault troops sealed off whole quarters and scoured the neighborhoods street by street. Before Ana María traveled to Spain, she and Cristina removed their books from the house, secretly, and a friend of theirs, Vincente, buried them in someone's backyard.

Of course, they opposed the government and the military, and they helped those who were persecuted as best they could, but they had no compelling reason to join a party or to take up arms. Gisi, on the other hand, was much more involved. She was also much more intelligent. And her active concern was not something she put on for show, it was not insincere; it had always been in her, even when they first met. Her eyes grew narrow, out of empathy, out of indignation when she saw ragged children begging. That is just how she was. Without affectation, incidentally, without frivolous posturing. She never put on makeup. She didn't need to. She declared her political ideals only when it was necessary. It would never have occurred to her to do otherwise. She respected the opinions of others. She never tried to convince anyone that her view of the world was the correct one. In this regard she was quite restrained.

Sometime toward the end of seventy-five, or the beginning of seventy-six, Helga asked the girls if it would be all right if Gisi sent them the letters that she wrote to her and Willi. Of course! They handed over each letter to Gisi's mother as soon as it arrived. It was as simple as that. In the meantime, Helga and Guillermo had become the YPF club doctors. The transfer took place at the pool in Godoy Cruz. Cristina had her own thoughts on the matter. Namely, the Montoneros must be in a bad way if Gisi needs our help in order to stay in touch with her family.

By the way, Ana María Moral was also a good swimmer, especially in the two-hundred-meter butterfly. She competed for Talleres, the other large swim club in Mendoza. Her nickname was *La Pescadito*. Little fish. Too bad that only real fish can take permanent refuge in the water.

If Gisi had survived, she would have become a world-class scientist. A specialist in her field and a wonderful human being. She was not naive. She was not forced to do what she did. She knew precisely what she was risking. She had made it her cause, and it is not easy to accept the fact that it cost her her life. So many years have since passed, but Cristina and Ana María will never forget the results of that junior championship meet.

Gisi swam for Cristina although she was actually one level below her on the junior team. Cristina was considered a heavy favorite at the one-hundred and two-hundred-meter breaststroke, but she was unable to compete because she had had an appendectomy. Gisi was in great shape, and she outswam her competitors, who on average were four or five years older. This time, when the trophy was presented, Gisi showed no sign of embarrassment as she had at previous award ceremonies. While the spectators were still applauding, she jumped from the podium, ran over to Cristina, and handed her astonished friend the trophy.

For the real winner, she said, because you would have won if you had entered.

XIV
Mendoza, Argentina
1965

The arguments between Gisi and Heidi came to an abrupt end when the older sister entered secondary school in 1965. It was as if Heidi had waited to find a place where her behavior was not constantly at odds with the moral principles and expectations at home. She continued to be uninterested in politics, preferring to think about her wardrobe, and spent time with her friends whenever she could. She no longer needed to hide her test papers among Gisi's. She chose to major in the humanities, which would then allow her to work as a teacher without having to take additional courses. In the final two years of study, students concentrated on pedagogy, teaching methods, psychology, and logic. She was interested in everything that had to do with personality formation and the education of children. She even did well in mathematics and in the natural sciences. However, she was disappointed that most of her classmates were girls.

Two years behind her, Gisi completed elementary school in December 1967. She toyed with the idea of attending an agricultural school, *Liceo Agrícola* and passed the entrance exam. But she also passed the entrance exam for the very demanding technical college in Las Heras and decided to enroll there.

From the beginning, Heidi was like a second mother to Mónica, the baby of the family. Helga was often not home during the day because of her studies and her work, so it was natural that the older sisters changed Mónica's diapers, helped her get dressed, combed her hair, picked her up from the day care center and later from school, and accompanied her to birthday parties. But more than that, Heidi enjoyed taking responsibility for her sister who was seven years younger, to give her some attention, and, when needed, to order her around a bit. Even today she still finds it difficult to accept the fact that Mónica has her own life; she has to force herself not to give her orders, or at least not to offer all kinds of advice. For her, Mónica has remained the little sister who had to be home by eight and whose clothing she sniffed to detect whether the *hermanita* had secretly been smoking cigarettes. And Mónica admits that it was Heidi, not Helga, who can best recall her earliest years—and also that, as a child, she was intelligent yet especially dreamy. *Vivía en la luna terriblemente.* Mónica had her head in the clouds and let her thoughts wander, just not to where she was, in a poorly equipped classroom for example, in front of a teacher who took it as a personal insult when a child failed to pay attention during her class, and who yelled at her. Willi and Helga met with the teacher and requested that she try to show more patience instead of terrifying their daughter with her angry outbursts. Because the request proved futile, they decided it was better to make a change even though Mónica was only in the first grade, and they enrolled her a few months later, in June or July 1966, in a different school. The new teacher, a woman from their neighborhood, said to Heidi, listen, your sister does not even know all the letters of the alphabet; if someone does not take the time to practice them with her, she'll have to repeat the grade. So during the school vacation, Heidi drilled the alphabet into Mónica's head for two weeks. That was not a burden for her; she was thirteen at the time and was already convinced that there was nothing better than working with children.

Gisi's relationship to Mónica was different, more intimate, like a friendship between girls that is not affected by time or circumstances. The difference in their ages was also rather considerable, five years, but it expressed itself only to the extent that Gisi was similarly intent on taking care of her little sister. In contrast to Heidi, she made it clear that she needed Mónica as much as Mónica needed her. In hindsight, Mónica sees the period between age five and twelve as a time of uninterrupted happiness that was above all the result of Gisi's attention. Gisi was, she says, many things in one: companion, friend, advisor, role model.

And I am still searching for her, in every pair of blue eyes, in every head of blond hair, in every smile that comes my way on the street or elsewhere.

She and Gisi—Mo and Gi they called themselves—invented and mastered a secret language that simply doubled the first syllable of each word and that they alone could speak. As they rode their bicycles around the block, they took turns coming up with a song and singing it for at least ten minutes; they told each other jokes that they made up, did somersaults until they were dizzy, walked on their hands along the edge of the YPF swimming pool, jumped rope until they dropped to the ground exhausted and exuberant, because they had miscounted, and rolled in the grass. And if they hopped on the bus, hungry and sweaty after practice, and found two seats, and no seniors got on the bus (since Gisi would always jump up and offer them her seat), if they could then sit there all the way home, Mo laid her head on Gisi's shoulder and fell right asleep, while Gisi sat still next to her. She would even try to use her body to compensate for the lurching and jerking of the bus, and only shortly before they reached the bus stop where they were to get off did she wake Mo up.

At home, in the room they shared, they moved their beds together because they still needed each other's closeness, and they tickled each other until their stomachs hurt from laughter and pure joy, says Mónica. Once, they painted their room together and decorated the walls with orange and brown triangles. It looked fabulous, and Mo's classmates were amazed; they envied her because she had a sister who was her best friend. Mónica says that even when Gi was already with Alfredo, her first and only boyfriend, Gisi stood him up more than once because she would rather play with her.

It was also Alfredo who accompanied Gisi when she had to put her dog Lucky to sleep. He was a Pekinese that was originally given to Heidi as a present, but later Gi and Mo took care of him until he lost a leg when he ran out onto the street one day and was hit by a truck. The veterinarian thought the dog should be put to sleep right away, but Mónica protested. She sobbed, don't kill him, he can live with three legs, so they gave him water all night long; feebly, he licked their hands, without raising his head or wagging his tail. The following morning Gi took Mo in her arms and carried her to bed. Go to sleep, don't cry. Alfredo and I are taking him away. But why? Because he wouldn't have a life any more.

XV
Mendoza, Argentina
early 1970s

Her relationship with Alfredo had begun years earlier, namely when Heidi was thirteen or fourteen years old and a student at the secondary school. She has since forgotten where and how she first met him. He did live in the same quarter, twenty blocks away, so it's possible that one of her friends had brought him along. Alfredo was a month or six weeks older than Heidi, wiry, black-haired, of Creole heritage, and he really wanted to go out with her. Just the two of us, without the others. Heidi, who in her wildest dreams never thought about a long-term relationship with a boy, could not get rid of him easily. She was happy to be flirted with; everything beyond that was a little creepy. But Alfredo did not give up; again and again he repeated his request. Out of the blue he would appear on the street. He even showed up at her house one day; the only way to avoid meeting him was to have her mother tell him that she was not available: Alfredo is on his way over here again, please tell him that I'm not home. After two or three failed attempts, he gave up.

Four years later, 1970 or 1971, Heidi cut school one day. She was walking with a girlfriend across the *Plaza Independencia* and heard someone call her name. When she turned around, she stood face to face with Alfredo.

What a coincidence, after so much time, I am so pleased to

have run into you, so, may I come visit you? You still live in the Calle Juan Jufré, right?

Yes, said Heidi, still there. It's good to see you too, how are you doing?

Actually, she did not want to know. Alfredo had excellent manners, he acted like a gentleman. That bothered her; she preferred boys who occasionally got carried away, who pulled the chair out from underneath someone; in other words, high-spirited guys. Alfredo was mannerly, boring. While everyone else greeted her with a kiss on the cheek, he just put out his hand. *Hola, mucho gusto.*

Then I may see you?

All right, Alfredo.

And at the same time she wondered how she would get rid of him again.

Of course he was at her door the next day.

Will you go out with me? No, today doesn't work for me.

Then tomorrow.

That's also not good.

Friday?

At some point she no longer had an excuse.

OK. But you have to bring a friend, someone whom my parents know, otherwise they won't let me go. (A white lie; Heidi had long ago determined that she would go out with whomever she wanted. But her father did warn her not to take up with someone in the military or with a divorced man.)

When Alfredo picked her up, he was accompanied by a boy from the neighborhood, a childhood playmate. They all went dancing, and hardly had the other boy disappeared into the melee, when Alfredo ordered pink champagne, to mark the occasion, as he said, to drink to her finally having agreed to go out with him. She did not know where to look, certainly not into Alfredo's black, smitten eyes, nor did she know what to do with her hands. Her answers were monosyllabic, which was unusual for her. But her reticence did not prevent him from trying to make a second date right away.

But this time really only the two of us. How about next Tuesday?

Heidi tried to buy some time. Again she told him a lie, that her parents did not let her go out alone with a boy.

No way. Well, only if my sister could be there, so there would be two couples. If you can find someone for her, . . .

I made it damned hard on him, says Heidi. It was as if I had said: If you can dress up as superman, then I'll go out with you. A ridiculous precondition. Besides, he didn't know Gisi because she was always in her room studying whenever he came by.

My sister, you, another boy, and I. Or we can just forget about it.

OK then, Tuesday, and I'll bring a friend along. At eight, does that work for you?

Now Heidi had to win over her sister.

Gisi, you have to help me, this Alfredo is mad about me, but I don't like him. I don't want to be alone with him. I swear, he's serious. He'll stick his tongue in my mouth the first chance he gets; I don't want to have anything to do with him. I can't even bring myself to shake his hand; can you come along, just this once, he promised to bring another guy.

And my sister, says Heidi, did me this great favor. OK, she said, I'll come along.

The fourth member of the group was Oscar Mussuto, whom Heidi and Gisi met for the first time that evening. Oscar was tall, had broad shoulders and was a straight shooter; his ancestors were Italian immigrants from Sicily. His father had died three years earlier. At seventeen, Oscar had to take over the family business, and he has been in the car business ever since. Heidi thought he was an all right guy; in any case there was no comparison to Alfredo, whom she still did not like.

So, she and Alfredo, Gisi and Oscar. It was not the only time they went out together. On the third or fourth date Alfredo got behind the wheel of Oscar's car, and when he tried to park it, he scraped the curb or hit the car in front of him. Heidi does not recall the details, but the damage was not great: the car had a few scratches or a small dent, and there was no further talk about it.

But at home that evening, Heidi said to Gisi: poor Oscar, now Alfredo has damaged his car.

What do you mean, poor Oscar. He was at fault; he distracted him. And anyway…

What—anyway?

I'm just saying…

Does that mean that you like Alfredo better?

Gisi nodded. Heidi was astounded.

You know what, she said after a short silence. Let's just switch. Because Alfredo and I, honestly, nothing will come of it. I don't know Oscar well, but I like him better.

How do you imagine this happening, asked Gisi. We can't just tell them, hey, what do you think, let's swap partners, she's with you and I'm with him.

Just let me take care of it.

The next time they went dancing, Heidi waited for a chance to be alone with Oscar.

Look, I don't know whether you can talk to your friend about this, the thing is, I'm not interested in him, but I don't know how to get that across to him. I'm afraid I might hurt him.

And because he did not answer right away, she thought that he felt deceived. To salvage the situation, she said: To be honest, I like you a lot more.

Those were my exact words, Heidi says. Since then Oscar has been claiming that I seduced him. But really, I only wanted to get rid of Alfredo. And it worked. I don't know how Oscar arranged it, but when he picked us up the next time Alfredo went straight to Gisi, and it was clear to us all that the deck had been reshuffled. We drove to the *Parque San Martín;* it was a weekday. And I said, Gisi and I can't stay out too late tonight, we have school tomorrow and we have to get up early. We took a walk under the trees, Oscar and I were out ahead, and the other two walked behind us. Everything was quite innocent, the distance between us grew greater and greater, and suddenly my sister and Alfredo were no longer in sight. To be honest, I was totally bored with Oscar and imagined that Gisi was just as bored with Alfredo and would be mad at me. In any case, I wanted to get home as quickly as possible, but we couldn't find the two of them, so I began to worry. Not excessively, because in those days you could go walking, even at night, without fear of being mugged, but I was concerned. If something had happened, it would be my fault because I had convinced Gisi to do me a favor. I couldn't believe my eyes when we finally found them. They were kissing, and Gisi was totally beside herself, like in a trance; and it wasn't easy getting them into the car. Oscar drove and I sat next to him, the other two in the backseat. When I dared to look in the rear view mirror, they were kissing again, or still, in a tight embrace, and looked totally disheveled. I was flabbergasted. More than flabbergasted. At home Gisi was in seventh heaven. That was the beginning of their relationship. They got along very well with each other. I never saw or heard them argue, no comparison to Oscar and me.

So, Alfredo. Alfredo Escámez. Born on May 25, 1953. (Not true, says Heidi. He was born some days earlier, at the beginning of the month, but his mother entered that date in the birth registry because whoever was born on the anniversary of the Argentine Declaration of Independence was excused from military service.) Schoolboy. Later a student at *Universidad Tecnológica Nacional*. Taxi driver. Union member. Member of the Peronist Work Youth. Montonero. Missing since October 27, 1976.

XVI
Mendoza, Argentina
1970s

Miguel Mancuso also attended the technical college in Las Heras. He was in the class ahead of Gisi, and so he did not notice her until he sat down across from her on the first day of classes after the break. He was repeating the third year. She struck him as very shy, and she quickly turned deep red when she felt embarrassed. At the same time, she was the best student in the class, in mathematics a genius, he says, astute and able to pick things up quickly, the pride of all the teachers, unafraid of confrontation when she believed that a fellow student had been done an injustice. But she attracted Miguel's attention not only for these traits but also because she sat next to Elba Maure, and the contrast between the two students was striking. Gisela was tall for her age, blond, and shapely while Elba was somewhat plump, short and dark with pitch-black hair. Gisela was quiet; Elba could talk your ear off. They probably got along so well because of their differing temperaments.

It was a question of feelings, says Elba. I am an extrovert, and Gisela probably liked that. In Mendoza the people are less outgoing.

In her first year at the university, Gisi also became close friends with Liliana Vargas, whose oldest sister lived near the Tenenbaums, which is why she often took a detour to the Calle Juan Jufré. The girls studied for their tests together, and

Elba and Gisi were supportive of Liliana. She benefited from their diligence. The two of them patiently explained to her what she had not understood in class.

At first, Miguel had little contact with Gisi. He had the impression that she was not that interested in boys. Only in the course of the following school year did their temporary proximity in the classroom develop into a tender friendship. Sometimes they went dancing, to the Calatrava, a bar in the center of town: he with Liliana, Gisi with José Álverez, another student. To Miguel's horror, Gisi was crazy about Tom Jones, whom she found particularly attractive both for his voice and his good looks.

For me, says Miguel, it was British sentimental schmalz. He was a singing vacuum cleaner salesman, who was never quite able to button up his shirt. In Argentina, political songs were the rage, and Gisi was wild about Tom Jones!

Without meaning to, he became her masculine confidant. A kind of brother, although he really would have liked to be more to her. One day she confided to him that she was attracted to José Álverez.

Can't understand it.

There is nothing to understand. I just like him.

She was very empathetic and loving, Miguel says. Besides that, we were at an age when our antennas were up anyway, registering everything that occurred or could occur between boys and girls. And she just happened to like José Álverez. They probably kissed a few times, nothing more.

Miguel was instantly taken by Willi and Helga: with the seriousness with which they discussed problems that were rarely raised in other families and with their curiosity about what young people were thinking. To him they seemed like they were from another world. He was also impressed by their modest lifestyle. Along the way they had acquired a sputtering car that was ready for the scrap heap; Willi drove it in a most daring manner. When they visited their patients, however, they still just hopped on their bikes or went by foot.

Elba recalls that classical music could often be heard in Gisi's home. That was uncommon; so too, it appeared to her, were their open and frequent conversations about politics, during which her parents never used their own more expansive life experience as a basis of their argument. Helga served them milkshakes; these too were not available anywhere else.

Gisi was raised in a completely different manner from the rest of us, says Liliana. Not in a liberal way—even if there were no restrictions on her freedom—but rather in a spirit of mutual trust. For example, at thirteen she already had her own key to the apartment. We couldn't imagine that even in our dreams! Or, when the school principal asked her parents to come to his office to discuss her alleged misconduct. Guillermo told him that he and his wife had no reason to listen to possible allegations and that their daughter was fully capable of justifying her own behavior.

It's possible that the complaints of the school principal may have had something to do with the student strike during their final year at school. The students were required to wear a uniform to school, brown pants or a brown skirt, a white shirt, and a brown bow or a brown tie. But the principal suddenly decided that the students should wear a sky-blue uniform, the color of the Argentine flag. For the parents, who by and large were from modest backgrounds, this arbitrary decision was an additional burden; it was already difficult to scrape together the money for the uniforms. The result was a bitter con-frontation, in which Gisi was a participant, between the school administration and the student government. It ended with Gisi's snubbing of the principal at her graduation ceremony. She had received three awards: best pupil in the class, best in mathematics, and most congenial classmate. When she was called to the podium to receive the medals, she shook hands with all her teachers, but not with the principal.

It is also possible, however, that the principal's summoning of her parents to discuss Gisi's behavior stemmed from another conflict. Both Helga and Willi maintained that the man was obstinate, authoritarian, and a real Nazi both in his mentality and in his leadership style; he never missed an opportunity to track down recalcitrant pupils and punish them. Once, says Elba, he made them stand at attention in the blazing sun for hours on end because during the long recess they had jokingly made off with a cow from a neighboring dairy farm and had milked it in the school courtyard.

In general, the students had a good relationship with their teachers, most of whom worked at the university, either as part-time or full-time lecturers. They demanded a lot from their students, but they also sought to communicate their knowledge and to show its practical application. The chemistry class, for instance, was occasionally held in one of the buildings of the Ministry of Economics; the students tested for food safety, of course at no pay. Miguel recalls three female teachers who gave them an opportunity to express their own unformed opinions and quixotic ideas about how the world might be configured. There was Mrs. Soria who taught history; she allowed them to discuss current political events: the abduction and murder of General Aramburu, the operation that had first brought the Montoneros to the attention of the whole country; the social unrest in Mendoza and its bloody suppression; and the union's demands, as expressed on the flyers that were distributed outside the factories and at the universities. Then there was the literature teacher, Gringa González, who made clear to them that works of art always contain the conditions that give rise to them. On occasion, she also played the songs of the Spaniard Joan Manuel Serrat, which, according to Miguel, facilitated discussion and built consensus. And Mrs. Bobillo, the geography teacher who encouraged them to do group work on topics such as inflation, monopoly, and the gross national product, which were fascinating for young people who had just begun to perceive that social conditions are constructed and subject to change, says Miguel.

The school was no breeding ground for political activism, but we knew what we were talking about. Especially Gisela. Gradually José Álverez and Elba too. Less so Vargas. This is when I really got to know Gisela. She was a diamond in the rough for me. She had everything it takes to become a free person. That was not the case with Heidi; true, she was attractive and uncomplicated, but somehow shallow. There was good chemistry between Gisela and me; we understood each other even without speaking. That is why I was pretty distraught when Alfredo showed up at her side. I had the feeling that he took away some of her independence. I asked her once, why do you let others influence you? Why are you following the crowd? Why don't you think before you become involved in something? She made excuses: spirituality is fine, but you also have to be active. Not the same old Christian morality again, if someone hits you, you should turn the other cheek. That's not for me, she said. But I did not hold to this Christian notion. If you are going to live with the pack, you have to learn to howl with the wolves. And that is what happened to Gisela. She was in search of her identity, of a community in which she could grow, one that would give her some warmth. That is the way it is with people. I don't see anything objectionable in it. In defending others, Gisela put theory into practice.

Like Gisela, Miguel was close to deciding to become political. At the beginning of the seventies, everything seemed so clear: people on the right wore uniforms, those on the left had long hair. Twice he was stopped on the street and taken to the nearest precinct where they cut off most of his hair. The *gorilas* both hated and feared Perón. That was reason enough to be a Peronist. The Montoneros, who had only a small following in Mendoza, made an effort to recruit people. One day Gisela went to Miguel's home and brought along a stack of newspapers, *El Descamisado*. He distributed them, albeit reluctantly. Alfredo tried to win him over to the organization, as did Gisi. At her request he even picked up a contact from Buenos Aires at the bus station. The man's name was Tito; Miguel didn't know anything more about him. He brought him to the hotel and accompanied him to his room, where he pulled out a handgun. Miguel said to himself, this is not for me.

I kept my distance because I didn't want my parents to get into any trouble.

And because he thought he had more to gain from

mystical experiences, as well as from self-discovery and individual enlightenment. Even as a sixteen-year-old, he had begun to grapple with the teachings of the Armenian esoteric, George Ivanovich Gurdjieff, who in his Fourth Spiritual Path had held out the prospect of individual holistic growth through the harmonious development of one's feeling, thinking, and bodily movements. Then he studied the writings of the so-called American Knights of Fire, a sect (or movement, as Miguel says) that aspires to an expansion of consciousness through renunciation; because they sought to place their own followers in positions that opened up in the factories and ministries, they have become more widely known, albeit controversially, as *secta de los economistas*.

Liliana was also not happy that Gisi had fallen in love with Alfredo. She had known him earlier, casually. He and Oscar Mussuto had a tutor for French from whom she also took lessons. Liliana says that the two of them were quite lazy. It is hard to imagine that one of them would have such a great influence on Gisi five or six years later. For her, Liliana, it was Alfredo's fault that her friend withdrew a little. And when she did go out with her classmates, she did so alone, without Alfredo, who did not much appreciate her friends. He was somewhat authoritarian, *un tipo machista*. Liliana believes that he did not allow Gisi much freedom.

Elba has a different opinion.

Gisela and Alfredo were an ideal couple, she says. They were very compatible. They complemented each other wonderfully.

Take, for example, the final class trip to Córdoba, says Liliana, at the end of their last year at school. We had saved the whole year for the trip. Gisi too. But then she did not come with us. She told us, she did not want to go. Alfredo didn't want her to.

That was in 1973. The following year Miguel was drafted into the military. At that time the army was gearing up for a veritable campaign against the Marxist Revolutionary People's Army, which was waging a tenacious guerilla war in Tucumán. The government declared martial law across the province and issued a decree that provided the military with the rationale to crush the insurgency by any means. After he completed his military service, Miguel wanted to study medicine. His parents were opposed to the idea: why had they made it possible for him to study chemical engineering if he wanted to start all over from the beginning? They refused to support him financially. He held out for half a year, then he packed his backpack and headed for Córdoba. He found work there with a company that had won the contract to create the land registry for Catamarca. While he was in boot camp, he lost contact with Gisi and Alfredo. He heard that they had gone underground. In April 1975 he happened to run into Gisi on the *Plaza San Martín*.

She looked terrific. But she appeared harried. It seemed to me that she was afraid of something.

At the end of the year Miguel returned to Mendoza where, at the home of his former teacher, Gringa González, he made the acquaintance of Stella, a young woman whom he married ten months later in October 1976. Gringa González surrounded herself with her high school and university students (mostly female) who on the weekends fanned out to the areas where the poor lived. Miguel recalls how they once worked to renovate a filthy, dilapidated school in the countryside. He also remembers that Gisi was present at two of the meetings of the group some time between November 1975 and March 1976.

We sat in the yard at the home of Stella's parents, passed around a bottle of wine, played guitar, and sang songs by Daniel Viglietti.

After that, he only saw her one more time. Elba too would see her friend once more, two or three days or a week after the final meeting between Gisi and Miguel. And of course Liliana says: if someone needs help, then you have to risk something.

XVII
Mendoza, Argentina
1970s

Truth be told, if she were in Alfredo's mother's shoes or his father's or of those of any other family member, Heidi would be really angry at Gisi and at her parents. But the opposite is the case; they adore Gisi, even today. That said, it is undoubtedly true that it was her sister, Gisi, who got Alfredo interested in politics. A youth from the outskirts of the city who was no different from a hundred thousand other youths from those parts, his father a laborer in a cement factory, his mother a seamstress, a sister who became a teacher, an outstanding teacher by the way who deserves to be a school principal, which she some day will be. With her husband she is active in the Rotary Club, which would cause her brother to turn over in his grave. And Gisi apparently seemed like a beam of light to this politically naïve, average family; a girl, hardly nineteen, who was elected president of the student body in her first year at the College of Engineering, where almost all the students were male and where the right wing set the tone. She easily passed all her exams and worked part-time in a lab while Alfredo worked as a taxi driver, doubted if he really wanted to be an architect, sought the advice of a counselor who was friendly with Heidi, and even after taking an aptitude test still did not know what he wanted to do. In short, a boy who had no clear goals. Nevertheless, if she, Heidi, were Alfredo's mother, she would resent Gisi for having drawn him into politics, even today. But, no, not at all, no hatred, no reproach, not a trace of ill will.

Only a few months ago Heidi was stopped by a young woman in front of a school. Did she have a moment? Heidi cannot stand to be accosted immediately before a counseling session; she needs her peace, to catch her breath, to gather her strength, before she is pestered with all kinds of questions and complaints by exhausted and underpaid teachers. Besides, as usual, she was arriving at the last minute; the principal was already sticking her head out the door.

Not now, said Heidi, I am totally stressed out, but if you are a teacher, I can make an appointment with you for an individual session.

It won't take long. It's a personal matter.

That's what they all say.

Okay, what does it involve?

I am Nenucho's cousin, said the young woman and looked at her expectantly.

Whose cousin?

Nenucho's.

It took Heidi a few seconds to comprehend whom she meant. Alfredo. At home they had called him *nene*; when he grew up, *nenucho*, his nickname, stayed with him.

I found his driver's license when I was cleaning up, said the woman. I don't know what to do with it; then I thought that perhaps you might have an idea. Besides that, I wanted to tell you that your sister is doing well. I see her almost every day. I could bring you some photos of her if you are interested.

O God, she is totally nuts, thought Heidi.

How old are you, she asked.
Twenty-seven.
Then you cannot have known my sister.
But I meet her regularly. She has not changed a bit.
Look, said Heidi, here's my card. Call me. I really have to get going; they are all waiting for me.

After this meeting, Heidi nearly collapsed. It is not every day, after all, that someone speaks to her about her sister and even claims that she is still alive. She reproached herself for having given the woman the card with her home address and telephone number. I should have given her the one with the office number, she thought. Now she might show up at my home some evening or call late at night and talk my ear off. Heidi did not even mention the encounter to her parents; that would be like rubbing salt in a wound. But whatever she intended, Alfredo's cousin's crazy talk is typical of the high regard in which his family members continued to hold Gisi. If they were Catholic, they would long ago have built a candle-lit shrine to her. Heidi never understood the reason for it. Perhaps—(warning!) she would not want to be misunderstood, she really does not have any prejudices – perhaps it has to do with the fact that they are all *morochos*, dark-skinned, black-haired, of non-European ancestry, and then suddenly Nenucho has a blond, blue-eyed, attractive young woman at his side, educated, community-minded, always prepared to help but without a hint of arrogance, charitable but without condescension. She does not know what her sister did with these people, but they are fully convinced that Gisi's presence was the best thing that ever happened to them. And that is why they never wonder whether Alfredo would still be alive if it had not been for

Gisi. Then it occurs to Heidi that she did in fact see Gisi once more, after she had come for a visit when Paola was three months old and had mistakenly or intentionally taken her comb.

It was noon, a weekday. Heidi had to get back to school right away, to teach. And there was Gisi and their mother. The two of them sat on the sofa, and her sister was crying. We loved each other very much, she said. And cried. And her mother tried to comfort her. And she, Heidi, sat alone at the table and stuffed food into her mouth. Later, in therapy, she often observed herself doing that. How she bent over her bowl and ate, not knowing what she should say, having only three thoughts: I have to take care of myself. I have to go to work. They are waiting for me. She could not manage in this decisive moment to become her sister's ally. It was the only time that she saw Gisi cry. That Gisi permitted others to see her so desperate. Because Alfredo had recently fallen into the hands of the military and because she knew that they would kill him or had already killed him. Then she added that he had saved her life – because the house in which they had been living was not stormed until a few hours after he was arrested. Clearly, Alfredo had not revealed anything although it was certain that he was horribly tortured. Because of him, no one else in their group had their cover blown. How did he do that without betraying anyone? To protect them all, especially her sister, who sat on the sofa and sobbed, while she, Heidi, took one bite after another, and chewed, and swallowed, and said only three sentences - as if her life depended on it all.

There had been a time, earlier, when she and Gisi avoided one another. Neither liked what the other was doing. Gisi was probably still going to school, her last year, and she herself had begun to study psychology. Besides, she was going out with Oscar who was terribly jealous and sensed a rival in every sexually mature two-legged being. She also had no real desire to spend time with the people that Gisi brought home. She was suspicious. All this secrecy. Telephone conversations that did not seem to make sense. Meetings late into the night. Agitated voices coming from the living room or the terrace, and whenever she opened the door, everyone suddenly went silent. It was about politics, that much she understood, and it made her angry. In the middle of it all, Gisi and, of course, Alfredo. He was practically a family member, much to the dismay of Grandma Laura who was spending her final years in Mendoza with her son and daughter-in-law. Laura Tenenbaum suspected that he wanted to live in their house, but she was only able to confide her fear to her oldest granddaughter. Willi and Helga cut her short whenever she mumbled something about a black bug. Gisi was clearly too headstrong for her; you couldn't tell her anything, and Mónica would have repeated any disparaging remark to her favorite sister.

Heidi did not take Oscar home very often. She was seldom home herself. She felt a sense of security with Oscar, and that was important to her. Politics did not promise that kind of security. Gisi lived in one world, she lived in another. For her, the question was never how to achieve justice for all, but, for example (and more importantly), how to have a fulfilling sex life or how to avoid an unwanted pregnancy. By that time she had already lost her virginity.

It was crazy that we did it, she said to Oscar. I am the

black sheep of the family. If I get pregnant now, my father will hang me from the nearest lamppost.

Her mother had warned her: this young man comes from a traditional family. If you sleep with him, he will walk out on you. I hope you know what you have to do.

My sister, Heidi told Oscar, would never do something like this, not before getting married.

Oscar laughed.

I saw her come out of cheap hotel with Alfredo.

That's a lie, said Heidi. You're only saying that so that I don't feel guilty.

OK, don't believe me, he said, but I saw her with my own eyes.

XVIII
Mendoza, Argentina
1972-1974

Willi and Helga pursued their study of medicine conscientiously. But they did not run themselves ragged either. Helga did not pass the physics exam at the end of the first year and was forced to sit out the second year; Willi then also decided to take a break from his studies so that they could stay in the same class. Six or seven years later he failed an obstetrics course, and this time it was Helga who waited for him. In between those years and even afterward they had to interrupt their studies several times due to financial constraints, until they finally passed the last exam on May 3, 1972, together. It took another year before they were awarded their degrees during which time they took courses in the *Hospital Central* and became certified in general medicine, surgery, pediatrics, and obstetrics. They immediately opened a practice on the ground floor of their home on Calle Juan Jufré. The front room was turned into a waiting room, and they shared the other room. Willi worked there as a general practitioner and Helga as a gynecologist. From the very beginning there was no dearth of patients.

During this time, in mid-1973, Perón returned to Argentina. In September 1955, seven months after Gisi was born, he had been removed from power by a military putsch and hounded into exile. To the Argentinians his absence coincided with the demise of the country: a series of dictators, interrupted by two short periods of democratically elected presidents who succumbed to the pressures of the military even before their terms expired. National sovereignty was undermined by the acceptance of the security policies of the United States which dictated that the enemy was to be pursued and combated within the country, that is, among its own citizens. It also meant that economic independence was lost, because the ruling elite failed to implement agrarian reforms, to modernize cattle production, and to promote the development of heavy industry with the proceeds from the exports. At the end of the sixties, moreover, the government reduced import duties and raised bank interest rates way beyond normal international rates; while this favored short-term investment, it offered no incentive to build new manufacturing plants. The Argentine industries suffered as a result of the cheap imports; unemployment rose, and step by step the welfare state was dismantled.

From Spain Perón increased his influence over the events unfolding in Argentina. Consciously catering to both sides of the political spectrum, he promised the right a corporately organized state that would neither interfere with the free flow of capital nor alter the existing arrangements with respect to property and privileges; he encouraged the left to take up arms against the domestic oligarchs, the foreign corporations, the corrupt union officials, and the repressive security forces. His assumed goal of *socialismo nacional* was so vague that both wings of his movement could be satisfied. For the one group, it meant that the general wanted to reform the country on the basis of national-socialistic principles; the other group felt confirmed in its belief that an independent path toward socialism was being pursued, one that would take into account the country's unique situation. The increasing societal pol-arization as well as the acts of violence carried out by forces that indiscriminately invoked his name paradoxically encouraged members of the various social classes to accept the view that only Perón himself would be able to put things right.

The election of March 1973, in which Perón was not allowed to be on the ballot himself, was won by his candidate Héctor Cámpora, a member of the left wing of the party, who wanted to transform the country through a program of social reform. But only a few weeks later Péron used the events of June 20 to encourage Cámpora to resign, and after early elections he ascended to the presidency in October. During his term in office, and even more so under the presidency of his widow María Estela Martínez, the extreme right was given free rein to move against the revolutionaries in its own ranks.

On that June 20, 1973 some three million people made a pilgrimage to the international airport in Buenos Aires to welcome Perón as he returned from exile. In the course of the celebration, *pistoleros* sitting in the stands of the union bosses fired into the columns of the Perónist Youth Group. The Montoneros returned fire. The "Ezeiza Massacre" ended with thirteen dead according to the official count, but more careful estimates indicate that at least 350 people were killed. The breach between the president and his leftist followers became clear on May 1, 1974, two months before Perón's death, when he banned the *jóvenes imberbes*, the beardless youth, from demonstrating on the *Plaza de Mayo* in Buenos Aires.

Willi and Helga never trusted the tricks of this authoritarian politician. They also thought very little of his prematurely deceased wife, María Eva Duarte, whose social-revolutionary legacy the Montoneros wanted to follow. In any case, they were immune to the religious fervor that was still accorded Perón and his chief propagandist. In this regard they also differed from most of the parents of the young people whom Gisi brought home. Nearly all of them had been studying for two years or more at the *Universidad Tecnológica* where Gisi was majoring in electrical engineering in early 1974. What united them was the irrepressible will to change the social conditions, the belief that the majority of the people would accept this change, and the certainty that they were living in a historical moment that obliged them to bring about this change. They were all in agreement that Argentina and, who knows, the whole continent, could be rebuilt from the ground up within a short time. Even the political disasters in neighboring Uruguay and Chile could not diminish their confidence. Perhaps they were encouraged by their own children who, while they had the capacity to live intensely in the present, were also able to recognize the powerful import of what they were imagining. They believed that they understood the dangers and that time was short, yet unlimited. Short with regard to the required effort and the obligations that they imposed on themselves; unlimited because they felt they could combine all the diverse interests that they had committed themselves to: university studies, politics, work, love, friendship.

The group was formed in 1972. That was when the *Partido Socialista Popular* (Socialist Peoples' Party) emerged out of an amalgamation of several leftist parties that had sought a fusion of the interests of the workers and the middle class. Their leaders believed that the proletariat was represented by the Peronists and that the middle class was represented by the Radical Citizen's Party. Therefore, for the upcoming elections, a mutually acceptable candidate, one who could represent the two political camps under a socialist umbrella, had to be found. The young socialists in Mendoza opposed this arrangement, first, because they knew that neither the Peronists nor the Radicals could be moved to accept such a deal, and, second, because they were convinced that there was as yet no organization in Argentina that represented a particular class. Because of their opposition, they were expelled from the party. Under their new name *Partido Socialista de Vanguardia* they did not achieve any greater relevance even at the local level. Only at the *Universidad Tecnológica* did the group find a following because their student organization, the *Agrupación Universitaria Popular*, did not limit itself to political protest actions but also made seemingly more ordinary demands such as the need for a student dining hall.

University politics was not enough for them. They began to examine national socialism from the ground up, and they devoted themselves to the study of the history of Argentina. They also traced both the dualism between agrarian production and an export economy as well as that between the poverty in the countryside and the exclusive maritime wealth in Buenos Aires back to their historical origins, i.e., the period before independence. Gisi participated in this reading group. With her questions and objections she repeatedly embarrassed Alejandro Dolz, the political leader of the group.

But her criticisms were never intended to harm anyone, he says.

She did not want to appear self-important, says Cristina Coll, who also participated in the reading group.

She only tried to get to the bottom of things, says Mili Vernet, the third member who survived.

She was open, says Cristina, like we all were, open and in search of a way that accommodated contradictory points of view.

Because the time had not yet come when strict discipline was demanded of us, says Alejandro. The risk was reasonable when we began to be politically active, and later when the sides hardened their positions, the group fell apart.

It was the best time of our lives, says Cristina.

From a political perspective, says Alejandro.

With respect to living together, says Cristina, we shared everything.

Like brothers and sisters, says Alejandro.

Like comrades, says Mili.

Like friends, says Isa Navarro, who is Mili's wife.

We drove off to the countryside, pitched our tents somewhere, and went swimming or rock climbing, says Cristina. We also had parties, sang songs, laughed hard and often, so that Mónica still thinks that we only concerned ourselves with politics on the side. She was almost always there.

Once, three of us pulled her out of the water, says Mili. Gisela, Alejandro, and I. Mónica was swimming and suddenly found herself in a whirlpool, so we formed a human chain and pulled her out.

And we loved Gisela's parents, says Cristina. The easy

atmosphere in their home. I was educated in convent schools. Mendoza was absolutely a religious swamp, sexuality a taboo. But not in Gisela's house. I remember once that Guillermo told her: At least take the condoms off the table before your little sister comes home. It was the kind of joke that we laughed at and whose punch line made us envious because that would never have happened in our families.

We all would have liked to have such parents, says Mili. The respect that they accorded us. Everyone could learn a lesson from them.

The same goes for Gisela's character, says Cristina. How honest and reliable she was. I think she was the best person that I have ever known. She was absolutely sincere. She seemed incapable of lying or giving an evasive answer, even once.

She did not say much, says Mili, but what she said was meaningful.

She wrote a lot, says Isa, and when one hand grew tired, she continued with the other.

A faded, green T-shirt, that's what she usually wore, says Cristina. She did not need to attract attention to be happy.

There was an angelic aura about her, says Mili. Alfredo was also OK. A buddy, a friend, who kept his word. But he did not have this aura. He was the daredevil type; she was the reflective one.

Both of them, as if in a fairy tale, says Cristina. "Beauty and the beast."

It was only through Alfredo that I got to know her, says Mili. Our student group was having a meeting, and afterward she came to pick him up. She was still attending school at that time. Next year I will be your *compañera*, she said. And she was. More than that. Cristina and Alejandro were right: the time we had with Gisi was the best time of our lives. Then came the period of fear, terror, and loss; the period of lies and isolation; the period in which we tried to get some firm ground under our feet. We are actually still in that phase.

I used to think that our deepest relationships resulted from extreme situations. Because we are dependent on each other. But now I've changed my mind, says Alejandro. I believe we had the most intimate friendships while we were part of the group. And it wasn't an extreme situation. We did not have to hide. It was an explosion of creativity, the discovery of a new world, and we found it together. At least in our heads. And in our hearts. And at the worst possible moment. Because the putsch in Chile brought the beginning of neo-liberalism. But we didn't know that then. Not even Gisi knew it.

XIX
Mendoza, Argentina
1974-1975

The group disbanded on a warm spring day, one that would not be followed by a carefree summer. The meeting was held, as usual, at Gisi's place, according to Alejandro and Cristina, and Mili remembers that two or three days before or after their last gathering a clandestine press conference was held in Buenos Aires at which the Montoneros announced that they would immediately be going underground again because of the increasing repression by the state. That was on September 6, 1974.

It was already clear to them that they could no longer continue to operate as they had. For months they had been discussing the possibility of whether they could integrate their views of socialism into a party or movement that was strong and viable enough to implement them. Or at least to entrust them to a party that might acquire this capability even if at the moment that party lacked relevance. They could think of no other solution. To simply wait, look on, and continue to talk without trying to influence the course of history seemed like betrayal to them.

It was a hard-fought and passionate debate. But they were able to avoid humiliating one another. And when they all went their own separate ways after four or five hours, divided but not estranged, they did not feel a sense of satisfaction or relief that they had made the right decision. No rejoicing on the part of those who had unequivocally favored collaboration with the Peronist Youth Group or support for its electoral platform, the Authentic Party; no dejection on the faces of those who were in the minority. Instead, a trace of melancholy, a faint foreboding that something good had been irretrievably lost. *La vida no fragmentada*, as Cristina labeled it, the unbroken life, in which the present did not need to be sacrificed to the future, nor private happiness to the pursuit of communal welfare.

Gisi and Alfredo had favored joining the Peronists as had Mili, Isa, Mili's friend Nacho Mamani, *El Flaco* Osvaldo Rosales, and the quiet José Galamba. They had argued that the struggle for social hegemony was taking place within Peronism. Without it, there could be no change, and within it the dispute among the various strands was still unresolved. They wanted to strengthen the left from within. Alejandro Dolz, on the other hand, thought it illusory to believe that Peronism would ever grow into a national liberation movement. It was too riddled with reactionary and even fascist elements for that. The better, the only choice was to join *Poder Obrero*, a Leninist organization that was not corrupted by either the populist contortions of Peronism or by the reformism of traditional leftist parties. But only two or three of their friends agreed with him, and Cristina followed Alejandro to *Poder Obrero*, not out of inner conviction but just because she was his girlfriend.

We were deeply depressed after the meeting, says Alejandro. We didn't think that their path was feasible.

It signified a rupture, says Cristina.

The first big loss, says Alejandro. Apart from that, they were right. More precisely, they were less wrong than we were. What they hoped for did not occur. But it could have occurred. It was still possible. Our cause, on the other hand, was doomed from the start. What was *Poder Obrero* anyway? Three dozen revolutionaries with no prospect of a revolution.

Willi saw it that way as well, even then. Gisi had convinced him that there was no way around Peronism. The people are on our side, she maintained; the people who don't want to have anything to do with you, replied Willi. But he himself recalled that freedom fighters everywhere had always been in the minority; his skepticism was only intended to prevent her from becoming foolishly overconfident. Of course, he shared her ideal of a socialism that grew out of its own national particularity, in contrast to one that was imposed on a people. He was proud of her, but he thought it important not to show his pride. He did not object to her participation in the Peronist Youth Organization, which was seen as particularly radical. It was inconceivable that he would try to dissuade his daughter from doing something that they both thought was right. Besides, neither her studies nor her work suffered from her political activism. In the morning she taught mathematics, physics, and chemistry at a private school; in the afternoon she attended lectures, and in the evening she took part in the training courses. In the early morning or between these commitments she distributed flyers. She still blushed every time Mili asked her what her grades were after an exam. Nine out of ten in Mathematical Analysis I, nine in Technical English, ten in Applied Chemistry, eight in Physics I, ten in Statistics.

The atmosphere at the universities was less volatile in Mendoza than in Buenos Aires, Córdoba, or La Plata. According to Willi that had to do with the fact that most of the students there still lived at home, under the supervision of their parents who did not want to have anything to do with politics. At the *Universidad Tecnológica* the situation was different because many of the students were already a little older, more mature, worked during the day, earned money, and did not have to rely on anyone else for their support. On the other hand, there were right-wing extremists, goon squads, and informants at the university who passed on information about dissident students to the police. Heidi once heard her sister say that she and a few other girls, as they were on their way to a demonstration or a rally, sometimes intentionally stumbled in the stairwell and latched onto a stranger for support. In this way they could quickly and inconspicuously determine if the young man who was rushing up the stairs next to them was carrying a pistol under his jacket. Heidi was outraged not only at the fascists but also at her sister for deliberately throwing herself into a dangerous situation. She was equally outraged when Gisi insisted one day that she immediately stop greeting her if they happened to meet on the street or anywhere else outside the apartment.

Whatever you do, don't call me by my name, she said. Do you get that, *Colorada*?

No, I am too stupid for that, said Heidi, as she jerked her head back, put on an arrogant face, and simply walked away from her. At the same time, she wanted to tell her sister off. Just as she did the woman in Gisi's youth organization who studied psychology with her and who kept asking her to participate in this meeting or that demonstration.

Just leave me alone with your damned meetings. I don't want to know anything about them. It would be better if you sat your butt down and cracked the books!

Mónica, on the other hand, interpreted Gisi's precaution as a game. I'll never be able to do that, to refrain from calling you by your name, she said; so they agreed to simply swap the short-hand versions of their names: Gi was immediately Mo, and Mo was Gi.

That's how it was in 1975, Gisi's second year at the university, when the country was sinking into chaos. Perón's widow surrounded herself with ministers and advisers who were ardent believers in astrology, the ordering hand of the archangel Gabriel, and the efficacy of free-market shock therapy; they sensed the sulfurous stench of Marxism everywhere and declared the existing contracts between workers and bosses null and void. In June, after a tremendous devaluation of the peso and exorbitant price increases, real earnings fell, on average, sixty percent from one day to the next. For the first time the Peronist trade union called for a general strike against its own government. The army leadership refused to take action against the strikers; it preferred to wait it out until no one would be interested in defending the corrupt national leadership against a revolting military.

In the preceding year a new university statute barring all political activity at the universities had gone into effect. Since then sixteen universities were 'intervened', that is, placed under the control of the government, four thousand professors dismissed, and sixteen hundred students arrested. And the *Triple A*[4] death squads, which were organized by the

---

[4] Triple A refers to the Argentine Anti-Communist Alliance.

minister for social welfare López Rega, had begun to hunt down oppositional unionists, students, and intellectuals. In Mendoza they were considerate enough to head out on their murderous campaigns only once a week, on Friday evening. Many of Gisi's comrades spent their Friday nights with friends or outside of the city, under the night sky, in the mountains. Because Gisi was now attending evening lectures that did not end until shortly before midnight, Willi waited for her at the bus stop every Friday night.

It is pointless to ask what induced her in August 1975 to join the Montoneros. The line between Peronist Youth and Peronist guerrilla was rather fluid; there were no ideological contradictions, and the essential differences—those between political and military structures, and those between the renunciation of force and the use of force—became insignificant as society in general was militarized. The one group did the groundwork for the other, rented cars or clandestine apartments, obtained documents or hid pamphlets and weapons, ran errands or gathered information that was useful to the Montoneros for their surprise attacks and assaults. Mili's group once got an order to gather information on the daily routine of an administrative secretary at the *Universidad Tecnológica* who was known to coordinate the activities of the right-wing shock troops. For a week they closely watched his house, duly noting when the man, his wife, or their children left, when they returned, when the maid arrived in the morning, when she went shopping, and when she took the bus home. A few days later a commando blew the roof off the house. No one was injured.

In those days, Mili says, life as a Montonero was exciting,

like in a novel. We in the Youth were just as vulnerable as they were. The risk was the same for everyone. With one difference: they also had the sense that they were on an adventure, acting like a kind of Robin Hood.

That Gisi would have been enticed by adventure is out of the question. Mili, Isa, and Nacho recall that she was always quite fearful. Afraid of being harassed, abused or tortured.

She had a very child-like way about her when she expressed this fear, says Isa.

We too were afraid, says Mili, every one of us. But the events broke over us like a wave and swept us along. Although we knew what could happen, we thought about it less and less.

But what did remain a part of us, says Nacho, was this instinct, like that of an animal before an earthquake.

He and Mili are convinced that Alfredo influenced Gisi's decision, or at least anticipated it; he was the first to join the Montoneros, impulsive as he was.

They didn't discuss it with us. They didn't ask us beforehand what we thought of it.

Gisi also presented it to her parents as a *fait accompli*. Helga was very much alarmed when she found out about it: we have decided to join the Montoneros. No particularly strong effort to hold her back. Even today Helga asks herself whether she shouldn't have tried to break her daughter's will. But how could she when it was she who had taught her to respect the will of others? Helga says she felt somewhat paralyzed the whole time.

To be under the illusion that most Argentinians had a favorable opinion of the Montoneros was one thing; but Helga was more terrified by what Nacho called *la precondición de matar*, the willingness to kill, which moved him and Mili not to follow Gisi's example. Willi had always strongly opposed physical violence; he condemned the possession and purchase of firearms. He refused to even pick up a pistol or a rifle. He never hit his children. He was living proof that it was possible to deal with your adversaries and with unfavorable conditions through ideas and words alone. Gisi pointed to the brutality of the security forces, and Willi was not able to refute her argument that the Montoneros were forced to defend themselves if they did not want to be quickly killed off. There was no longer any authority to turn to if you suffered harm or injustice. It was all only a matter of life and death now – and of a noble goal.

We supported her, says Willi. No question about it.

Besides, they were absolutely right, Helga says, a hundred percent. They foresaw what would happen and tried to prevent it: that the other side wanted to turn this country into a colony for the corporations.

Whether their struggle paid off? We will know in a hundred years, says Willi.

XX
Mendoza, Argentina
1976

Tuesday, February 10, 1976, marked Helga and Willi's twenty-fifth wedding anniversary. Laura Tenenbaum had reserved a table in the most elegant restaurant in the city, Bodega 900, for the following Saturday to celebrate the silver anniversary of her son and daughter-in-law in stylish fashion. The small party included her grandchildren and of course Oscar and Alfredo. Willi bought a tie with a flowery design, and Helga had a dress made for the occasion, which would close one chapter of their lives and open another, for Heidi and Oscar had been married the previous year and Heidi was now six months pregnant. And Gisi and Alfredo intended to get married before the end of the year.

But the dinner had to be cancelled. Helga never got to wear the dress, and for a long time she felt more like crying than celebrating. It was not until nine or ten years later that Heidi dared to congratulate her parents on their anniversary again, cautiously handing her mother a small bouquet of flowers. Helga said, it would be best if we could eliminate this date from the calendar because it was the worst day of our marriage, to which Heidi replied, for me it was a happy day because if you two had not found each other, I would never have been born. A few more years passed before Helga and Willi were able to go out again on their anniversary and pose for a few photos, only the two of them or along with their surviving daughters, sons-in-law, grandchildren, and their first great-grandchild.

The tragedy occurred shortly before noon. Alfredo showed up unexpectedly and asked Willi to come along saying that the military had stormed the apartment and that one *compañero* had been injured in the encounter. Willi got up from the table, grabbed his medical bag and with his long strides followed Alfredo. He sat in the passenger seat. During the ride he looked down at the floor mat or into the glove compartment. Even when he got out of the car, he kept his eyes down as he walked behind Alfredo toward the house. These were normal precautions that would prevent him in an interrogation from being able to specify the route or the hiding place.

When Willi returned home two hours later, he told Helga that the injury was not particularly serious. The young man he treated had sprained his foot when he made a sudden movement. Willi was more concerned about the boy's frame of mind – he was depressed, felt guilty because the military had carried off his wife or girlfriend in the raid while he hid in the courtyard behind some boards or a barrel. With hesitation the boy explained how a soldier had found him but had not betrayed him; he had wanted to get up, but the soldier suddenly turned around and walked away.

An unbelievable story, said Willi.

That was on Tuesday, says Helga.

On Friday they learned from the fiancé of Alfredo's sister that the authorities had searched and ransacked the home of the Escámez family. He further reported that the military was looking for Alfredo, who was fortunately not at home — just so you know. That meant that Gisi could no longer risk coming home, and that they too had to be prepared for a raid. But none came, for reasons about which Willi and Helga could only speculate; there was a captain or major living in their neighborhood who had always been kind to them, and perhaps he had made sure that they were left alone even if their residence was under surveillance from now on.

Only afterwards did Heidi learn that her parents often treated wounded and sick Montoneros, out of solidarity, kindness, or loyalty to Gisi. They were even put on alert when a precarious operation was about to take place, and under the pretense that they were making house calls to the sick, her parents relayed messages and offered their house as a hiding place. Right after her wedding Heidi moved out of the family home. But even if she had stayed, her parents would have kept their illegal activities a secret from their oldest daughter, for her safety and their own. Indeed, Heidi cannot remember whether her father was called to attend to an emergency on February 10. She was visiting her parents around noon that day. Or was it not until Saturday? While she was helping her mother in the kitchen, Gisi entered the room and said to her mother, Mama, it's time. I have to go underground. Right now. Heidi assumes that Gisi went to her room either before or after the conversation and put some clothes into her linen bag. Her mother wiped her hand on her apron for what seemed an interminably long time. Then all three of them stood there for a while, like statues. Numb. The sound of a dripping faucet could be heard. Or music from the radio. The twittering of birds from the terrace. But today is …, her mother said, we have the party tonight. Gisi only smiled. Please understand; the command reads: immediately, and then she did in fact leave right away.

Never to return again, as my mother says.

Six weeks earlier, on the night of January 3, 1976, a commando of Monteneros attacked police station number five in Codoy Cruz. The intended victim of the attack was an official who was both feared and hated for his horrific torture techniques; but one of his colleagues, a certain Alberto Cuello, who was said to have been a thoroughly decent man, bore the brunt of the attack. Cuello was mistakenly shot to death from a passing car, because on short notice he had switched shifts with another guard in front of the police station. Instead of reacting with concealed joy, as the assassins had expected, the people of Mendoza responded with horror and disgust. Alfredo had participated in the operation as the driver of the escort vehicle, a taxi that he had taken from the garage without his employer's knowledge. Perhaps someone observed him take it, or he was seen when he returned the vehicle. In any case, his boss accused him directly of having participated in the assassination. Alfredo denied it, but his boss made a dismissive gesture with his hand; he did not want to know about it, did not want to get into trouble, patted him on the shoulder, watch out, young man, too bad, we got along well with each other.

Do you think he will turn you in, Alfredo was asked by his cell leader.

Don't think so. Unless it all blows up and then they grill him.

For the time being, don't show your face at home. Does he know anyone else from the organization besides you?

No, said Alfredo. I mean, yes. He often saw me with my girlfriend.

Then she needs a safe place too.

The safest place that they could find for Gisi was the parental home of her comrade Lichi Larrea because a police officer often hung out there, Inspector Narváez, who was in charge of the intelligence service in Mendoza. It was rather unlikely that the house would be under surveillance without his knowledge. Narváez was married to Lichi's godmother; he had known Lichi since she was a young girl, and he was aware of her political activism and subsequent militancy. When three Montoneros were captured in her boyfriend's apartment in November 1975, he sent Lichi, as a precaution, to Chile for two weeks until the furor died down. She returned in December, and in January, around the twelfth, she was asked if Valentina could live with her. That was Gisi's code name, derived from Valentina Tereshkova, the Soviet cosmonaut who was the first woman to fly into space. Lichi and Gisi, or Valentina, had participated in the same training sessions; as delegates, they recruited new cadres at the university, and they also distributed flyers together a couple of times. They were mid-level operatives within the organization, according to Lichi.

While Lichi was busy during the day carrying out her political assignments, Gisi fully complied with the order not leave the house. Her comrade's mother enjoyed the unexpected companionship. The fact that Gisi used a code name and was surrounded by secrecy was irrelevant to her; she knew the girl with the close-cropped, blond hair from before, as a swimmer. Out of curiosity she asked her about her training methods and her triumphs as a highly successful athlete. She was touched by Gisi's demeanor, a combination of confidence and embarrassment. She was flattered when she saw how Gisi devoured her schnitzel, and she became a little jealous when her daughter came home and took her guest to her room. Gisi watched old movies on TV, played cards, and read Lichi's psychology books late into the night. She was grateful for the enforced idleness; here I can do things, she said to Lichi, that I never did at home. They talked very little about their respective assignments; discretion had long become the basis of all their communications. But at night, when they lay awake in their beds, they talked quietly about the things that troubled them and that fulfilled them: the desire to have children and to start a family, the family not as the nucleus of neuroses and bastion of the state ruled by one class, but rather as the smallest social unit in the struggle toward a great goal, for example. Or they talked about how each of them dealt with the ever-present danger—what strategies they developed, how they altered their behavior patterns, and what rules they internalized to avoid suffering the consequences of the risks they took. An especially pressing question: recently a few high ranking Montoneros—in Buenos Aires, not in Mendoza—had divulged some information either because of the threat of torture or because they were really tortured, and the covers of several hundred militants were blown. Even then it was touch and go in the organization, says Lichi, on the brink of chaos. Their leaders had hammered into them as the first commandment: *No entregarse vivo, resistir hasta escapar, o morir en el intento.* Do not surrender under any circumstances, resist and run away, or die while trying to escape. It is not known what Gisi thought of the cyanide capsule that Montoneros were always supposed to carry with them in case no escape was possible. Of course, Lichi says, she expressed her fears that something could happen to her and Alfredo. Lichi was optimistic; my old man is a musician, and so he knows everyone and everything. If I'm the target, he'll sound the alarm right away!

Ten days later the all-clear signal was given, and Gisi was allowed to leave the home of the Larrea family. She left Lichi and her mother with the same radiant but shy smile with which she had arrived. She heard that the investigation conducted by the authorities into the attack on the police station apparently hadn't gone anywhere. But barely three weeks later it turned out that the police had picked up Gisi's and Alfredo's trail.

XXI
Argentina
1975-1976

He'd rather not discuss his deepest concerns in the presence of his in-laws. Not that he has anything against them, or that he would dare to criticize them; on the contrary, they are two wonderful people with whom he gets along extremely well. He is after all their first and oldest son-in-law; he loves them dearly, and they love him because they know him, and they also know that he is who he is and no different. But if one could get the truth out of him, he would say that not everything in the family worked as it was supposed to.

First of all, he would recall the time when he made a play for Gisi, who was damned attractive with her sky-blue eyes, long legs and tantalizing little breasts, which does not change the fact that there was simply nothing between them because they were two very different people. Gisi had a strong work ethic. But that would not have been an obstacle, he would say; he had seen that in his own family. His father acquired a couple of houses through his hard work, but he did not think that he was better than other people. Three of his five children were able to go to college, and two others worked in business. The problem was really that Gisi was extremely intellectual and introverted—which was true—but he was not—which was also true—and therefore he didn't know what to do with her, and she with him. When they went out together, Alfredo with Heidi, he with Gisi, and a boy from the neighborhood named Alberto with a third girl, who has since passed away, it was really difficult to get Gisi to dance with him. She either did not listen to him, or she turned away, or was bored. She did not drink or smoke, while everyone else, including Heidi, smoked like a chimney, because that was part of growing up. It was quickly clear to him that he would not win Gisi. Maybe I have a chance with her sister, he told himself; I'll try for her. With Alfredo, it was just the opposite: no chance with Heidi, but perhaps with Gisi, so it made sense that they should swap sisters. Because, he would say, even in those days Gisi was interested in politics, and he wasn't. Not at all, not in the least. His ambition went no farther than taking care of himself and his family, hanging out with his friends, getting along with his neighbors, being independent of everyone, and not having to fear anyone. Gisi had a different mentality, who knows, he would say, maybe she and Alfredo were ahead of their time. He can't and won't judge that, but in any case he would have nothing more to do with them once he realized what they had got themselves into. Whenever he picked up Heidi, her house was full of people sitting around talking politics. That was not for him! And also not for Heidi, whom he won over to his side, which later led to some tension in the family; he believes, he would say, that his in-laws spoke badly of him for a while because he did not want anything at all to do with Gisi and Alfredo. It is understandable that they were angry. After all, Gisi was their daughter. She was his wife's sister. His sister-in-law. And he was new to the family. But he knew what was at stake, and the subsequent events proved him right: one day during the process, as the generals liked to call their dictatorship, "Process of National Reorganization," it was a Saturday morning, they already had a child, their oldest daughter, and he went to work after breakfast. So he walks out of the house, unlocks the car, gets in, starts the engine, is in a good mood, looks forward to the customers and afterward to lunch at his in-laws. But hardly has he turned the corner when behind him three guys are meddling with his apartment door. Definitely military or paramilitary, from a commando for special assignments even though they were not wearing uniforms; they neither said who they were nor did they show any identification. They just broke in. His wife was in the shower. Granted, they behaved somewhat politely, one guy threw her a towel, she was allowed to get dressed, and they did not lay a finger on either his wife or the baby. Heidi had to sit on the sofa and answer a ton of questions as the men searched the apartment, pulling out all the drawers and examining each and every book. Finally, they left, but not before announcing that they would be paying a visit to Heidi's parents that same day. He only learned all of this when he came home from work. The raid, he would say, nearly made him crazy with fear. At a time when you were at the mercy of these people anyway, he feared an assault, one that could be repeated at a moment's notice and might even be worse. That was his "view," he would say. At the time the only thing he had on his mind was to save his family, to prevent anything from happening to them, especially to his daughter, his first-born. The fear was not unfounded; it was later determined that many children were simply stolen. The parents murdered, the children stolen. That is why he wanted to know absolutely nothing of Gisi, who had got them all into hot water. That is why he was so annoyed when Gisi asked him if she could stay with them for just one night. No, no, and again no! Period. As if you are speaking to a stubborn child, who has not learned her limits, no, you may not do that, no, you can't have that even if you stand on your head. That's the way it is. I mean it. Yes, I'm sure. She was old enough to recognize the seriousness of the situation. He was, he would say, very angry at her. Because she placed his family in danger. And also a little angry at his in-laws because they simply stood on the sidelines. With all their relatives in Europe and in Bolivia, it would not have been hard to get her to some safe place. Then she would still be alive. If he had been her father, he would have simply packed her up and sent her abroad, regardless of whether she objected. Of course, I would have done that, he would say, if one could in fact get the truth out of him.

What he would say next, not in their presence, for he has too much respect and regard for his in-laws, preferably in his own house, alone, his wife and children also would not need to be present, what also disturbs him is that no one in the family speaks of Gisi. No one, not even his wife, despite the fact that she is a psychologist and has been in therapy for years. When Gisi disappeared, she became a taboo subject. No one spoke of her after that. As if there were something to hide. And no one considered her dead. Neither her parents, nor her sisters. He cannot understand that. He would have said from the very beginning, my daughter is dead. Or he would have denied her death, in which case, however, he would have said, she's alive, so I am going to look for her and will not rest until I find her! His in-laws are wonderful and admirable people, to be sure, but something is not quite right here. The silence. Because they feel guilty? Don't know, he would say.

He doesn't; he has no trouble saying that his sister-in-law is dead. Or disappeared, which is really the same thing. Because what did they do with the 'disappeared'? Dropped them into the ocean, or shot them and then dumped them in mass graves, not any different from what the Nazis did in Europe. For sure. And so they invented this word *desaparecido*, disappeared. But they are dead.

He would have talked about her, he'd say. Constantly. He would not have kept his mouth shut. Although, for a long time, the Argentinians, were afraid to open their mouths.

Only occasionally, each year on the fourth of February, does he hear his in-laws say: "Today would be her birthday." But that's all. Not one word about Gisi, about whether she would have married, whether her marriage would have been a happy one, whether she would have had children and how many, where she would live, what kind of job she would have, how she would act in this or that situation, how they would spend their time together. Not one word. As if she were neither alive nor dead, but hovered about, like a kind of angel, between heaven and earth. He doesn't think this silence is good, he would say. He sometimes thinks that it may have to do with his in-laws' country of origin, the quiet and reserved character of the people there. He knows Austria, a really wonderful country with quiet and reserved people, who are somewhat submissive, but well-bred, which can be clearly seen in the way pedestrians wait for the traffic light at the crossing. The Argentinians are different in that regard, loud and hotheaded, and always ready to protest. Although, under the military dictatorship, whenever they encountered the military on the street, they all kept their mouths shut and made an effort to look the other way. He did too. Because the others had their fingers on the trigger. What could they really have done? Boom!

That's what he would say. If someone were to ask him why talking about Gisi is a taboo.

XXII
Argentina
1975

Helga wishes that Gisi had had some bad luck. Bad luck in December 1975, when she was stopped by the police. If they had just arrested her, sentenced her, and locked her up because of her support for a terrorist organization or for making disparaging remarks about the Argentine military. Lord only knows what they charged Daniel Ubertone with, the boy who was handing out flyers with her. They dragged him straight to the police car. But in her case they seemed uncertain. Gisi was extraordinarily composed when there was danger either because of or in spite of her fear of being mistreated; she was also experienced at looking innocent, at appeasing aggressive types, and at rendering her own fear as cheerful equanimity.

It remains a mystery how she was able to get rid of the remaining flyers within seconds. Her shoulder bag was empty except for a crumpled tissue. The police officers demanded an ID. She only had the long-expired ID from the swim club on her. Or none at all. Or better yet the counterfeit one with her photo where she is looking straight into the camera and which bore another woman's name. In any case, quite unexpectedly they let Gisi go. They hauled Ubertone to the police station, then from jail to jail. Although they were not able to make a credible case against him for distributing the flyers, he spent more than seven years behind bars.

He survived, says Helga.

Just as Gisi would likely have survived if the police had not merely frightened her. Or if she and Alfredo, two or three months later, had not said no.

No, thanks. I appreciate your offer; that's really very decent of you, but...

If they had listened to the husband of Alfredo's cousin, who drove a truck to Brazil every few weeks. He wanted to hide them behind some sacks and crates and take them across the border. Of course, Brazil was a military dictatorship, but with some luck one could make one's way because things were easing up there, in contrast to Argentina where at three in the morning on March 24, 1976, the commanders of the army, navy and air force overthrew the government, dissolved parliament, dismissed governors and federal judges, abolished the right to strike, placed the unions under government control, and banned all activity by political parties.

Most people were relieved when the putsch happened. They now expected sanctions against the waves of violence and corruption, energetic measures to curb inflation and encourage economic recovery, and the restitution of the rule of law. The military junta held out just this prospect in a measured address to the nation, one which had even Willi and Helga hopeful that matters would be less harsh than they were after the last coup d'état, that of General Onganía in 1966.

Not even the Montoneros, especially not them, says Helga, were able to foresee the extent to which the military would wreak havoc. We were with a girl from Santa Fe, with Elsa Sedrán, she was the leader of the group to which Gisi belonged. Well, it doesn't look so bad, she said. But right away they just started killing them all, one after another.

In February Gisi and Alfredo had gone into hiding at his aunt's place, a few kilometers outside of the city. Even before the coup, they returned to Mendoza, perhaps on their superiors' orders, because a new offensive was planned, and it's possible that Gisi was brought in to consult about the course it should take. Or it became clear to them that her aunt's neighbors viewed them with growing suspicion, so they could no longer stay with her. Helga says that Gisi subsequently stayed with Liliana Vargas, and Heidi recalls that Alfredo and Gisi tried to spend the night with them once. Perhaps it was then, three or four days before the putsch, perhaps it had been weeks before. In any case, one evening they were at her door.

Colorada, let us in, we need a place for one night.

Heidi opened the door, made way for them to enter, locked the door behind her, kissed and hugged them, directed them through the hallway to what would become the children's room, asked if they had eaten, to which Gisi nodded, took some sheets and towels out of the closet, and placed them on the pull-out sofa. They spoke little because of the late hour; it was approaching midnight. Oscar had already gone to bed, and Heidi had opened the door in her nightgown. She noticed that Alfredo and Gisi also looked very tired.

Oscar created a terrible scene in the bedroom. Why did she let the two of them in? What was she thinking? Why hadn't she asked him first? Did she want to give birth to her child in prison? Oscar raged, Heidi sobbed, and it went on like this for quite a while behind the closed door. Despite their efforts to speak softly, their voices were loud enough to signal to the two in the other room that they were not wanted, because the next morning, according to Heidi, there was no sign of Alfredo and Gisi when she went to check on them. As she pressed down the door handle and carefully opened the door, she realized that they had left. They must have departed that very night since the sofa bed had not been slept in and the apartment door was shut but not locked. They had only pulled the door closed from the outside. Quiet, embarrassed, amused, or full of contempt? Because Heidi and Oscar had locked horns over them.

Gisi kept in touch with her parents and with Mónica through her friends from her school days. When something was urgent, she would call home even though it was assumed that the phone was tapped at least some of the time.

We were always able to arrange it somehow, says Willi. With tricks that were absolutely juvenile. When we set a meeting time by phone, it was always three hours earlier. When we agreed to meet at eight, then it was clear to both of us that we would meet at five. Or the meeting place, on so and so street, at such and such corner, then we knew it is ten blocks further up. Our childish trickery was effective.

But dangerous, before and especially after the military putsch. Twice Willi and Helga had to quickly go into hiding because the cover of some Montoneros who knew them personally and knew of their collaboration had been blown. It could be assumed that under torture they would reveal their names. Once, they were taken in by one of Oscar's brothers for two or three days; the second time they sought refuge in the home of Helga's cousin Trixi in Buenos Aires. Naturally they took Mónica along. Willi's mother remained behind, alone in the apartment; everything is normal, she said on the telephone, no, no one asked for you. A week passed, then ten days, and the same response. So they could then assume that Gisi's comrades had not revealed anything or that for some reason they were not seen as a threat. Or that they had a protective angel among the police or in the army. Possibly the neighbor mentioned earlier.

The coup d'état had a negative effect on their professional lives. In addition to their practice, they worked in the hospital: Willi received no compensation from the *Hospital Central*, and Helga had a permanent contract in the *Emilio Civit*. After he had taken two vacation days, Willi was barred from entering the hospital. Helga met the same fate in late September or October. Like all employees in the health ministry, she picked up her pay at the end of the month. When she opened the envelope, she found, instead of the bills, a letter informing her that she was terminated effective immediately. She protested to the relevant official, an officer in the military, claiming that she was entitled to at least her last month's wages.

Get out of here, he said, or I will have you arrested on the spot.

With Heidi it was just the opposite. She was not barred from her studies, but the university was closed down because of the students. People claimed that the psychology major had demonstrably fallen into the hands of the subversives. Fortunately, she was allowed to transfer to a private university; since she had only a few more exams to take, the institution generously waived her tuition fees. That she was allowed to complete her studies is ultimately due to Gisi, Heidi claims. Without her circumspection she would have certainly been thrown out. She knows of students who were expelled for minor offenses. To have Gisi as a sister was no small matter. She always took care to keep her identity secret, so that she, Heidi, would not suffer any disadvantages. That's why she never ended her letters with her signature and always left out the salutation. Always just *Colorada*, Red Head; *Feliz Cumpleaños, Colorada,* for example, in June on Heidi's twenty-fourth birthday, and many thanks for the gift, the cups are just what we need, they are our first.

When Helga brought her the card with the congratulatory message, Gisi and Alfredo had already been living in San Juan for two months, the capital of the province of the same name, located some 170 kilometers south of Mendoza.

One could assume that San Juan was more of a refuge than a battle zone for them. Like many comrades from Mendoza, they had been sent there by the leadership. They were now considered part of the military structure, actively involved in it; they participated in shooting drills in the remote *Cañadón Negro*. They manufactured hand grenades in a repair shop, set up weapon caches, and stole cars for their operations. Once Gisi told her parents about a fire fight, one that she herself, however, did not participate in.

She always told us everything. I mean, to the extent that she could. She was apparently not present for the armed fighting. She was responsible more for *agitación,* creating *notas* for factories and barrios.

She handed out flyers, covered walls with slogans against the dictatorship as well as appeals for resistance to the regime, and met with the members of her cell every day at a specific time on a specific corner. Going underground and surviving was hardly possible in Mendoza where the Argentine armed forces had achieved their avowed goal: to isolate the opposition and then to wipe them out within a few weeks.

Because of how the military combated terrorism, says Nacho, no one wanted to hide us in their homes. Neither our relatives nor our friends. And you can't endanger them. The moment quickly arrives when you no longer know where you will spend the night. You are absolutely alone. And doomed.

In San Juan Gisi and Alfredo had to rely on their own resources to cover their living expenses. There was no support from the organization, which in the early seventies had taken in massive amounts of money by kidnapping corporate leaders. But Willi and Helga, who visited them at least once a month, did provide support. They brought them a used refrigerator, then a washing machine, but the first thing they brought was a nebulizer for treating asthma patients. They also showed them how to give injections. Giving shots, administering inhalants, jobs with which they themselves had supported their own family for years.

As they had done in February when they visited their daughter at the home of Alfredo's aunt, they paid attention to whether they were being followed on the trip. When they were unsure, they reduced their speed, stopped for a break, or took a detour. In San Juan, Alfredo waited for them on a corner. He and Gisi lived in the center of the city, in a building that could easily be kept under surveillance. Later they were able to rent a house somewhat farther out of town, from which they could make an escape if the circumstances were right.

Mónica always went with her parents. She had cried and begged to come along when Gisi told them that she had received an assignment to go to San Juan.

Take me with you! Please! It doesn't matter where I go to school. I promise I won't be any trouble.

She rattled off a list of activities that she would do without complaint. Mop the floor, dust, shop, polish shoes, help with cooking, set the table, clear the table, wash the dishes, check to see if the coast is clear . . .

I'm sorry, but you just can't come with us.

. . . Hunt cockroaches, brew maté, fish the hair out of the drain, take the dog for a walk.

What dog, said Gisi sounding alarmed, at which Mónica had to laugh.

XXIII
Argentina
1976

Why don't you two get a dog, Heidi once asked, and at that time it was Gisi who laughed, disparagingly as if to say, you haven't got a clue.

I'm serious, a German shepherd, you can train him to alert you when someone comes by, and then you'll have time to get away.

Nonsense. More useful to us than a dog is a –

And Gisi used a word that Heidi had never heard before, three letters, one syllable, which she has since forgotten but at the time she asked what it meant, and someone told her, that's an automatic rifle.

I almost dropped dead. That meant that she had a house full of weapons. I was still naïve enough to believe that my sister would never, ever accept the logic of the others. In our family we were pacifists through and through – my father, my mother's parents, and my grandfather and his brother who had performed political street theater. To demonstrate, to strike, to free prisoners, whatever you like, but just don't stockpile weapons, or shoot the place up, or wage war! But in spite of all that, I never abandoned her. I always remained devoted to her. We never broke our bond with each other. That I never once traveled to San Juan says nothing about our relationship. I stayed home because there was no way that I would leave Paola alone. I wanted to take her along. Oscar wouldn't allow it. Not with the child. Go if you absolutely must. But our daughter is staying here! So I did not go. I gave my parents a couple of things for her, a heater, an iron because we had been given three at our wedding, some dishes, maybe some money, and whenever she wrote telling me that one of her *compañeras* was expecting, I knitted or sewed something, or I sent her the clothes that Paola had outgrown.

Two years later Heidi unexpectedly saw the baby clothes again. She and Oscar were living in a building that was owned by her mother-in-law and managed by Oscar. A young couple from San Rafael lived on the same floor, just next door. They had urgently needed an apartment because the woman was pregnant; they even agreed to pay six months' rent in advance. They said their parents advanced them the money. Apart from this unusually generous offer there was nothing suspicious about them; they appeared to work, because they left the apartment together in the morning, at almost the same time. The woman usually came home in the early afternoon and went shopping before she started dinner. Sometimes she would accompany Heidi and Paola if they went to play in the park. She said she was looking forward to having her child and wanted to know from Heidi if the first weeks after the delivery were really as exhausting as her mother had claimed.

Do you have what you need for the baby, Heidi asked one day when they ran into each other in the stairwell.

Oh, yes. Come in, I'll show you.

She smoothed out the blanket in her bedroom, and then she spread out the little shirts and bonnets and playsuits for Heidi to see.

Aren't they cute?

Heidi nodded and smiled; she had to make an effort not to let on.

That only happens in the movies, she said. That someone, while she's looking at a baby outfit, realizes the neighbor's secret. They were all things that I had once given my parents to take to San Juan.

It was also clear to her now why the woman had taken so long to open the door one evening when Heidi had already warmed Paola's milk and realized that she had no more sugar. She ran out into the hallway, knocked on her neighbor's door, and asked if she could borrow some. Then she heard a lot of noise, scraping, rustling, clattering, and whispering as if someone were cleaning up in a panic. A lover, whom she's locking in the closet because she thinks I'm her husband, Heidi smiled to herself. It's me, Heidi, and she knocked again.

It took a while for the woman to come to the door.

We were just moving some things around, she said. Did you knock?

They probably had a case of weapons or brochures, a duplicating machine or something like that lying around, says Heidi.

Two or three weeks after the unsettling recognition that she was living next door to Montoneros, Heidi was on her way home from a lecture around noon. When she turned onto her street, she saw men climbing across the roof of her building. There were also men in crouched position on the roofs of the nearby houses, holding rifles. Almost against her will, she continued walking; they've already seen me, she thought, if I turn around, they will suspect me. One of the tenants was standing in front of the building and looked in her direction. When she had just about reached him, he pointed to the roof and noted triumphantly: they're chasing hoodlums up there. Heidi walked by him without saying a word; she passed the front of her building and continued walking to the corner drugstore, where she asked if she could use the telephone. Just then a bus stopped outside; she ran out and got on.

Ten minutes later she was standing in front of Oscar.

There are *milicos* everywhere in our house, Oscar, do something, close the shop, get me out of here, we have to pick up Paola from daycare, I absolutely don't want . . . what if they have targeted us!

After he had calmed Heidi down and dropped her off at her mother's, Oscar drove slowly up his street. Through the windshield, then the side window, and finally in the rear view mirror, he took in what was happening. He immediately recognized one of the men who seemed to be securing the entrance; he was the friend of one of his cousins, a civilian, who to his mind would not have been capable of participating in a manhunt. He also recognized the couple from San Rafael as they were dragged out of the building.

First the husband. His wife stumbled behind him; they pulled her up by her hair.

In broad daylight, says Heidi.

Toward evening Oscar was able to convince her to return with him to the apartment. They learned that yet another neighbor had been dragged off, a young, single mother. Her two-year-old daughter, a particularly lively girl, often played with Paola, Heidi says.

The woman hauled off, the child shoved through a door to a neighbor. I would have gladly taken her; fortunately someone notified her grandparents, who picked her up a few days later.

Both the woman and the man from San Rafael were never seen again. We do know that the young, pregnant woman was thrust naked from a car a few days later outside the city, in El Challao. Heidi is convinced that the neighbor with the outstretched arm and smug attitude had something to do with it. That he denounced them. He denied it, and no one was able to pin anything on him. Later, Oscar reported one of the kidnappers, the friend of his cousin, to the police. Says Heidi. His name and everything. Unlikely that he was ever tried.

And then, much earlier, in their first apartment in Barrio Cano, something that Oscar also mentioned, one Saturday morning in September or October of 1976. Heidi was washing diapers in the bathtub. She was naked except for her bra, and Paola too was naked down below because she had some bleeding between the cheeks of her bottom. It was later determined that the culprit was a fungal infection, but at the time they thought that it was caused by the diapers, and so they followed the advice of the pediatrician to keep the chafed skin uncovered as much of the time as possible. That's why Heidi had only put an undershirt on her now.

She was in the bathroom with a bundle of diapers, and Paola was lying on the bed in her parents' bedroom. The chain lock on the apartment door was in place. Suddenly a grating sound as if someone were pushing with all their strength against the chain. Papa! called Heidi. They had agreed that he would pick her and Paola up for lunch. He was always so impetuous, slammed doors shut, and threw them wide open until they hit something, boom! And again boom! He will never break that habit, Heidi thought. Papa, I'll be right there, she called again. She stood up, turned halfway around, and looked right into the mouth of a revolver. It was presumably a revolver. Even today she does not know, and she does not care to know. She was so shocked at the time that although she had her ears and eyes wide open, she remembered nothing of what she saw and heard. She could not say anything; nor could she keep herself upright. She saw nothing but the revolver whose barrel was pointed at her face, and behind it a man, who briefly looked her over and then disappeared for a minute. He emerged again and threw her a bathrobe, maybe even the dress that she had carefully placed on the backrest of the sofa after breakfast so as not to wrinkle it. She cowered at the edge of the tub. Paralyzed.

It's always that way. When she is severely frightened, she goes weak in the knees.

The man took her arms, and, placing her left arm over his shoulder, dragged her out to the living room where two other men were waiting. Or just one? There he plopped her onto a chair. Where was her sister? When had she last seen her? Was she in contact with Alfredo Escámez? Where could they be found? They showed her photos of people that she was supposed to know. Heidi does not know what kind of answers she gave or whether she was able to answer at all.

The men searched the apartment, poked around in their papers, pulled out an old identification card from the *Centro Cultural Israelita*, asked whether she was still a member of the club, scrutinized the books on the shelf, one by one, but did not find anything illegal. Shortly after the putsch she had burned the diary of Che Guevara and Paolo Freire's *Pedagogy of the Oppressed* along with a few psychology books.

In the meantime the men brought Paola from the bedroom. She had begun to cry, but Heidi was still so shaken that she would not have been able to hold her. Paola would have slipped out of her arms, no, please don't! So the men had no other choice but to lay Paola in the crib where she presumably cried a while longer. Heidi can't recall. Only that she was not able to hold her child in her arms, and that the men asked her a lot of questions and had brought some tools that they set before her on the table. *Picanas* flashed through her mind, pliers or clamps to torture me with, electrically; perhaps they were only dictation machines, or weapons, one of the instruments appeared to be a weapon.

Finally, one of them discovered a violet stain on the floor. Printer's ink, that is our proof; you've had an illegal printing press here! And Heidi explained to them, haltingly yet in detail, how it came about, namely that her daughter's doctor had prescribed a gentian tincture that she, Heidi, had to apply with a thin brush to the skin in the anal cleft, and that one time as Heidi was applying it, Paola squirmed about and kicked the bottle. It fell and the tincture spilled out onto the porous linoleum, and although she wiped it up right away, she had not been able to get this stain out. The men seemed to believe her, but then they turned the apartment upside down again as they looked for a hectographed flyer. They stayed for an hour or an hour and a half, Heidi thinks, didn't smash anything, didn't tear anything to pieces, didn't scatter anything about, didn't mistreat her, didn't even threaten her. Then they packed their things and left the apartment.

They had hardly gone, when Heidi had her legs back again. She ran out onto the balcony to convince herself that the men had really left, and she watched them exit the building, laughing. They were not the usual thugs, they behaved in a relatively civilized manner; they were well spoken, moreover conventionally dressed, and as mentioned, Heidi remembers that they laughed as they departed.

She called Oscar from the neighbor's apartment downstairs; she was the only one in the building who had a telephone.

You have to come home immediately. Something terrible has happened. No, Paola is fine.

He was there in an instant, angry and relieved at the same time. Heidi's father pulled up shortly after him and got out of the car, but Oscar gave him a signal from the balcony to drive on, that he would explain everything to him later. Then he took Heidi and the baby to his mother's where they spent the rest of the day. Heidi says, she never wanted to go to the apartment again.

XXIV
Argentina
1970s

Longing for the best possible outcome. Working toward that goal. So that the door can open, their daughter can walk in, an angel from heaven can appear. For that, she would have had to leave the organization, at least once the Montoneros were officially banned. Renounce the armed struggle. That was a possibility, there were still a few days to mull it over, the decision did not have to be made overnight Heidi maintains. Opting out was no guarantee, but it offered a much greater chance to escape with your life. Take advantage of the material support of their parents, hide out with the relatives, in another city, stay off the streets for a year or longer, then find a job, as far away as possible, have a permanent residence, not too much contact with customers, business travel, few co-workers, in a lab, for example, for which Gisi had ideal qualifications. From home to work, from work to home.

This was not for Gisi. I remember exactly. I said: get out, there's still time. But she was too deeply involved in it all.

I can't leave my comrades in the lurch.

That was her answer. She was in charge of a unit. She felt responsible for her people.

I can't abandon them.

That was her answer to every other suggestion, to all her mother's requests. Only once, says Helga, was she prepared to go with us to Buenos Aires. Not for the long haul, but she would nevertheless have been relatively safe, at least for a short while.

I have to ask permission, she said. And on the next day: No, that won't work.

In Buenos Aires she could have moved in with Helga's cousin Peter who had a house that he used only on weekends. Pampas grass all around, seven shrubs, a laurel tree, a wall, the neighbors out of earshot. Tell Gisi, he had said, she is always welcome.

No also to the offer from her uncle in Vienna. Heinz Markstein had returned to Austria in January 1951 and worked as a journalist. He had fully expected Austrian society to have changed and that he would have an opportunity for professional advancement. But these hopes had been only partially realized and in a manner different from what he had imagined. He now came to Argentina for several days, and because Willi and Helga had arranged a meeting with Gisi during his stay, he went along to San Juan. He too knew the danger that his niece faced and suggested to her that she leave the country with him.

Come to Vienna. You can live with us and continue your studies at the university; as a fully trained professional you will be more useful to your country and to the revolution.

His second-oldest daughter was only four months younger than Gisi; he wanted to call home right away, have her passport sent to him, and then Gisi could easily leave the country. It would not have occurred to anyone that she was not the girl in the photo.

Thanks, Uncle Heinz, but I can't abandon my comrades . . .

To leave was to surrender, to give up on yourself and the others, the cause for which you are fighting as well as the obligation to remain truthful.

That's why Lichi Larrea also had not wanted to leave Argentina, under any circumstances. On the day after the coup her boyfriend was arrested at his job, the city transportation office. Inspector Narváez made sure that he was conditionally released the following Monday and immediately took him to see Lichi, to whom he held out three prospects concerning her future: "Either you wait here until they come to get you, or you turn yourself in. I could make an effort to get you over the border. As soon as possible. Otherwise even I won't be able to help you."

Neither, and I'm absolutely not going abroad.

Her boyfriend tried to get her to change her mind. He had been tortured during his arrest and through a hood forced over his head heard the kidnappers talk about how they raped women.

He's right, Lichi. Get out of here now; don't wait.

They were sitting or standing or pacing back and forth in the kitchen. The Inspector had insisted that they all come to a resolution: he, Lichi, her boyfriend, and her mother. No one else. They talked to her from seven in the evening until midnight. And Lichi still believed that it was precisely now that she had to stay and continue her work. Her mother sobbed. Her boyfriend begged her. The Inspector's patience was inexhaustible.

Ten days later Inspector Narváez called the travel agency and reserved two seats on a bus to Santiago, for Lichi and her mother but in his name. Lichi resisted until the end. Narváez and Lichi's father had to walk her arm in arm to get her onto the bus. Everything went fine at the border. In the Chilean capital mother and daughter took leave of each other. Lichi flew on to Ecuador where she could not shake the feeling that she had become alienated from her true self. Three-and-a-half years later she returned. Along with the first prisoners who were released from the dictators' jails, she founded a political group, *Intransigencia y Movilización Peronista*, whose name could have come from a hopelessly antiquated pamphlet.

That is the least of our concerns, says Lichi. In the group she made the acquaintance of Guillermo Tenenbaum. For a while he attended all the meetings, but then he stopped coming. She met Gisela's mother when her children became members of the swim club. The group still exists today. Lichi is certain that they will never achieve anything. But they continue even if just out of opposition to the individualism, as she says, the political individualism and the other kind, the herd mentality for individual happiness. She believes that Gisi would join them if she could.

Alejandro Dolz fled to Buenos Aires two days after the putsch. Cristina Coll followed him in September. Their first child, Sebastian, was born in November. In the same month Alejandro decided to break with *Poder Obrero*. The activities of the organization were now limited to attacks and violent measures of self-defense. They had no choice but to confront the military from a position of considerable weakness. The corpses of his comrades, or what remained of them, turned up in the Río de la Plata, chained to propane tanks and barrels.

Without the aid of Jewish merchants from the textile quarter Once, who let it be known that they had basically remained socialists, Alejandro would not have survived in the city, since he was without means to support himself. They gave him, without collateral and without a down payment, a large consignment of shirts, pants, and suits, which he then tried to sell as a retailer. Later he found work as a quality control inspector in a plastics factory and still later in a furniture storage facility. Cristina found employment as a graphic artist in an advertising agency and later with a newspaper for women. While their material situation gradually stabilized, they remained haunted by the fear that they would be discovered. For years they were forced to conceal from their neighbors and colleagues a part of their lives, a part without which they would not be themselves.

Whenever they ran into people from Mendoza in a café or on the street, acquaintances, even friends from their university days, which did happen occasionally, they looked studiously past them. They did not stop, did not greet them, not even a small gesture of recognition from table to table. For their own protection they developed an ability to compartmentalize their comments about their lives. Initially, hardly a day went by when they did not learn of some loss, someone who was shot, disappeared, or maimed. Outwardly, they did not appear to be affected. The sadness surrounding Osvaldo Rosales, when they learned that he was gunned down in front of his house and his body dragged away, even then Cristina could not cry. Of course, she had wanted to cry, she liked him, and the news was terribly painful. But there was this mechanism, to split herself into a Cristina who acted, another who talked, and a third who held back her tears.

She saw Gisi once more, in February 1977, in an ice-cream parlor in Calle San Martín, in Godoy Cruz. Helga arranged the meeting; Cristina had called to find out if it were possible to meet with Gisi again. She had come to Mendoza to show her baby son Sebastián to her parents and in-laws. It saddens Cristina that she can hardly remember the details. Was Gisi's hair dyed black? Was she wearing a headscarf like the women from the countryside do? Didn't she appear exhausted, depressed? Weren't the two of them, she and Gisi, more preoccupied with Sebastian than with each other? Wasn't he the center of attention because he distracted them from having to talk about experiences for which they had no words, or only abstract words, because they were terrified to admit that there was a chasm between them? Or wasn't it really the case that they shared an unspoken resentment at having been forced to grow up too quickly? According to Cristina, they didn't act like two women in their early or mid-twenties who matured more quickly than expected; rather, in this ice-cream parlor in the Calle San Martín, which could be raided at any time, they behaved like two little girls who would have preferred to play with dolls and only dealt with a baby because there were no dolls.

Isa Navarro and Mili Vernet escaped the henchmen by chance, with an instinct for the right moment, following a wild chase that ended well for them, even though they were traveling in a Citroën 2CV. By chance, because Isa was not in the office on the morning of June 7, 1976, when a couple of men asked for her. By instinct, because she immediately called Mili at the bank and because Mili, without hesitation, left the building through the back door while the commando that had been sent to apprehend him waited in the vestibule.

They were able to flee because the other vehicle did not start up right away, and so they had a two-hundred-meter head start. When they had shaken off their pursuers, they abandoned the car and fled on foot. For nineteen days they remained hidden in the apartment of a young married couple; on the twentieth day they purchased two tickets for Buenos Aires. They avoided the train station and hung out at a small, nearby plaza until the train arrived. Only when it started to pull out, did they run to the platform, jump onto the last car, and sit down in an empty compartment.

In Buenos Aires, Mili met with a contact from the Montoneros who wanted to integrate him into the organization right away. Mili was horrified by the recklessness with which they sought to confront the armed forces, without regard to losses. Nevertheless, he believes he would have participated in such a suicide mission had it not been for Isa. Her presence held him back not because she was against it but because he felt himself responsible for her. That's why he broke off all contact with the Montoneros.

It is the wrong decision no matter how you decide. You are unprotected outside of the organization. And if you stay within it, then you agree to follow the wrong path. When I made my decision, I had the feeling that I had abandoned them. I don't know what they felt. I don't know what Gisela would have felt.

Isa says that she understood the gravity of the situation only in retrospect. If she had been aware of it at that time, she certainly would not have become pregnant.

Their first child, Martín, was born in 1977. At least twice he saved their lives during a security sweep: because of his funny and trusting manner, they did not have to show their identification cards, once on a bus and again in a restaurant. The second child was born three years later.

We convinced ourselves that if it were a girl, then our friend must still be alive. It was a girl. We called her Gisela.

For a long time they did not tell their daughter how she came to have this unusual name. They wanted her to have a carefree childhood, without the burden of disappointed hopes. It may or may not be coincidence that this Gisela, who also dedicated herself to swimming as a teenager, was radical in her political beliefs, severe with herself, and incorruptible in her assessment of others.

Would Gisi have been able to tolerate inner exile, which required a lack of authenticity? Isa and Cristina, Mili and Alejandro could never honestly answer the questions: why they left Mendoza when they did, this jewel of horticulture, viticulture, and the natural beauty of the Andes, and moved to the hectic capital with its unhealthy climate; why they never returned to visit relatives or to spend their vacation in the mountains; where they actually knew each other from; or why they had broken off their studies. Again and again, they ran the risk of getting caught up in their own web of lies. That's why they withdrew, did not make new friends, preferred to cling to each other, they and eight other couples from Mendoza, refugees in their own country, who only spent one day a week, Sunday, with each other and who only then did not have to hide their true feelings.

Nacho Mamani stayed the longest in Mendoza. After the new regime had fired him from his job at the Department of Transportation, he found work helping to build a new soccer stadium, in which two years later the final rounds of the World Cup were played. Although he was no longer active in the union, his circle of friends grew ever smaller. In November his brother was abducted; he himself would have been next. In December 1976 he escaped to Buenos Aires.

I'll take you with me, he said to Gisi.

Not without Alfredo, she replied.

On March 6 of the same year, when it was clear that they would be sent to San Juan, Gisi and Alfredo were symbolically married. Such a thing happened more than once among the Montoneros, whose innermost core had been profoundly shaped by their Catholicism. They also counted several priests among their members, and because those who were persecuted could not be married either at the civil registry office or in a church, they secretly took a solemn oath in front of their closest comrades to love one another in good times and bad and to be faithful to each other. The exchange of their simple vows was also an occasion to get together with their best friends for a farewell dinner of bread, mortadella, and a few bottles of wine: Mili and Isa, Alejandro and Cristina, José Galamba and his wife Alicia, and of course the bridal couple.

Suddenly in the middle of the festivities, there was lots of crying, says Isa. Because it was clear to us that the road ahead would be very difficult, says Mili. Alfredo gave a speech. He said, we know what awaits us, never again will we be all together as we are today. Alfredo talked a lot that evening. Not Gisela. She was serious. You could see that she was afraid.

I was confident that she would survive, says Isa. Because she was always so well organized in everything.

XXV
Mendoza, Argentina
1976

Heidi was at her parents' apartment with Paola, who was lying in the crib, when the telephone rang. She picked up the receiver, and a voice, which she did not immediately recognize although it was that of her sister, said to her:

Colorada, they've got Alfredo.

No, she didn't say who it was, merely *Se lo llevaron al Negro*, and the *Negro* was Alfredo.

And then she hung up. Heidi ran into the kitchen and told her mother that she had just received a strange phone call. I think it was Gisi; something happened. Only when she repeated the sentence that she had just heard, did it become clear to her what it meant, and she ran back to the telephone to call Oscar and tell him to come get her right away. She absolutely had to get out of there, and take her daughter home; she wanted nothing to do with it all. Her parents would also leave with Mónica. Who knows for how long. No one could say what they would beat out of Alfredo.

On October 27, 1976, around noon or after lunch.

The second version is shorter, namely, Helga picked up the phone, and Gisi said to her: Alfredo had an accident, I'm coming to Mendoza tomorrow. Helga was terrified but did not let on. Rather, she answered with a calm voice, wait for us, we'll come get you.

Helga and Willi left for San Juan the next day, not by car but by train. Perhaps because the car was in the repair shop, or perhaps because Gisi had asked them to – it might get late and driving through the countryside at night could be dangerous.

Alfredo had been arrested during a *cita*, one of the many meetings that seemed to have only one aim now, namely, to determine who was still free and who had already disappeared.

It really should have been me, Gisi told her parents. He said, let me go, I know the boy, he's not been doing well since his girlfriend was arrested, maybe I can console him. So he went. But someone had informed the authorities of the *cita*.

When Alfredo still hadn't returned two hours later, Gisi left the house in a hurry. On the way she called the others, warned them, and passed along coded instructions. Somewhere she found a place for the night, and the next day she waited for her parents in a pastry shop.

She stayed only briefly in Mendoza, three or four nights, claiming that she had to get back to San Juan. Perhaps it was a matter of reorganizing or dissolving the group, assigning the remaining members to new cells. There was also an appointment that she absolutely had to keep. She took the early bus. Some hours later she informed her parents that she would be coming back since the liaison had not shown up. So, his cover was blown. She had been able to meet a few other *compañeros*, among them José Galamba and Ana María Moral who had given the military the slip. They had shot at Ana, but aside from a small wound to her lower leg she was unharmed.

And Alfredo? The authorities refused to admit to his parents that he was in the custody of the security forces. At some point, his mother found out that he had been tortured for a week in a police station in San Juan before he was transferred to Mendoza, presumably to the cellar of the police headquarters in the Calle Belgrano on the corner of Pedro Molina, where the secret prison D-2 was located. He had been seen at the airport. It's possible that they took him out over the South Atlantic or to a concentration camp in Buenos Aires or to the inconspicuous, poorly built shack, a few kilometers from the ski slope in Las Lajas.

He and Gisi had given some thought to the prospect that one of them might meet such a fate. In that case, each should feel free to make new plans for the future – to move beyond their happy memories together, to let go of their shared hopes for the future if need be, and to see someone else, without feeling guilty. More easily said than done. Who knows if Alfredo would have been able to do that? And Gisi? Her precarious situation would have prevented her from pursuing other relationships. Everything just continued as usual. That is not to say that she did not forge plans for the future, that she did not begin to create an existence without him. In the months leading up to her disappearance, when she was in Mendoza again, she would occasionally tell her parents: When all this is behind us, I'll finish my studies. Then I'll get my doctorate in chemistry. Or on a daytrip into the countryside when they passed tennis courts: I'd also like to learn to play tennis.

In August Gisi had collapsed on a street in San Juan. She had suddenly lost a lot of blood. A miscarriage, in the second month. Alfredo notified Helga, who immediately headed for San Juan. There was no danger; her daughter had a robust constitution.

You will both be happy that this happened, Gisi said.

Nonsense. Of course, we would have stood by you. But a child under these conditions.

Why should those sons of bitches be the only ones to have children? replied Gisi.

Her baby would have been born in March, says Helga. Then, besides our daughter, we would also have missed out on being with our grandchild.

They left San Juan on October 28 to bring Gisi back home. Willi at the steering wheel, and Gisi in the trunk of the car. Willi spent half the night looking for a place for her to stay. Everyone he asked had said no.

Sorry, Guillermo.

Doctor, we do appreciate you and your daughter, but you have to put yourself in our shoes.

The fifth or sixth address was the Cruz family. Mary, a friend of Gisi's from the swim club, still lived at home. Willi and Helga had become friends with her older brother Pancho. His mother, a conservative and affluent widow, did not even allow Willi to finish speaking.

Have her come in. She can stay as long as is necessary.

When Gisi left San Juan for the final time, she was determined not to be a burden on her parents any longer.

I'll find something, she said. Let me worry about that.

Miguel Mancuso says that one day in late October or early November, around seven o'clock in the evening, he heard a knock. He opened the door, and standing in front him was Gisi, alone, her pitch-black hair contrasting nicely with her light complexion, inconspicuously dressed, more like an older woman, with a knee-length skirt and wide jacket. He could not help himself: he hugged her passionately and swung her around in a circle. Then, carefully, he set her down on the ground and pulled her into the house.

His exuberance stemmed from the fact that he had thought she was dead; a rumor was circulating that Gisela had been fatally shot at a square somewhere in San Juan. He had not wanted to ask her parents, for fear of causing them unnecessary pain.

There were four people living in the house – he and Stella, the ceramic artist Fausto Marañón and his wife; all were thoroughly covered with paint because they had painted the walls that day. The two other housemates had also known Gisela, who looked tired and spoke very little. She asked him whether he could give her his identification card, which she apparently needed for someone else. He did not object because he was forever losing or misplacing his ID, and he asked her what Alfredo was up to. He thinks he remembers her saying that Alfredo had been killed. They talked a little longer over dinner. The four of them spoke of their intention to look for work in Brazil and, as soon as they had earned enough money, to travel to France. Miguel saw that their guest's eyes were falling shut. He and Fausto got a mattress from the storage closet. Stella spread a sheet over it, and in minutes Gisela was out like a light.

It was clear, says Miguel, that she was on a long trip.

The next morning, Gisi said her good-byes.

Stay a while longer. Rest for a few days, he said.

I can't, she said, they're after me. It's not safe enough for me here. I know of some other houses that are harder to find.

ARGENTINA'S ANGEL

What about your parents? Do you have anything you want me to say to them?

No, don't go to their place.

Those were the last words that I heard her utter. But you could see in her eyes that she was far from being defeated — that a fire still burned in her to push on.

XXVI
San Jose, Argentina
1976–1977

She must have shown up at Liliana Vargas' place on the same day. All the evidence, except for the hair color, points to that conclusion. Her hair was blond when I saw her; it was only later that she had had her hair dyed. This is confirmed by Elba Maure, who met with her friends several times in these days.

Liliana, too, went to the door when the doorbell rang; she was overjoyed to see Gisi again. They stood for a few minutes on the walkway in front of the house in the San José barrio where Liliana lived with her mother and three unmarried sisters. Gisi told her that she desperately needed accommodations. That she tried to stay with her sister and that her brother-in-law wouldn't let her into the apartment. Then she went to a former classmate (she didn't say who it was) and now to her, to Liliana.

She did not lie to me for a second. No deception of any kind, it is only for a few days. She even said, she could easily understand it if I said no, because she would not only endanger me but my whole family. But I didn't have to think about it for a second. I explained to my sisters that Gisi would be staying with us for a little while because her parents were busy doctors who were seldom at home and that she would at least have some company with us. Not a very convincing explanation, and they probably grew suspicious when Gisi dyed her hair black a few weeks later.

Are you crazy? We would love to have your curly blond hair, but otherwise they said nothing.

Liliana put Gisi up in her room; the windows faced the street. She wasn't working then, and so they could spend a lot of time together. In contrast to Liliana, who typically wasted half the morning sleeping, Gisi got up early; by the time Liliana awoke, Gisi had already been reading for a while, a weighty tome on economics. Every morning she carefully read the newspaper – look, here it says that three insurgents were killed in a fire fight, they are our people, and it wasn't a fire fight, they were shot in the back. Usually Gisi left the house in the afternoon or after lunch; she was back home again in three or at most five hours, in any case before it got dark.

Gisi paid attention to every noise from outside the house during the day and even at night when they weren't sleeping. It was not a bad thing that the room faced the front of the house; she would have noticed the approach of a commando early enough to escape through the courtyard and over the roofs. The houses were built close to one another, and Gisi was in great shape; at school she had been a top athlete—in running, broad jump, and high jump. She climbed like a cat; a wall was no obstacle for her. And Liliana thinks that she had a hand grenade on her. True, Gisi never showed it to her, and Liliana never rummaged through her bag. But her friend must have said something, otherwise she would not mention it now. And she suspects that Gisi would have killed herself before she would have surrendered. They had sworn to each other: better to be dead than to fall into their hands.

Once, Liliana wanted to take her to a family celebration—

a niece of hers was turning fifteen, but Gisi refused, saying that her presence would only endanger them all. Moreover, she would have had to put on a dress and high heels, and in such an outfit she would not get far if matters turned serious. In contrast, she was happy to accept an invitation to leave the city for a few hours when it was hot. They took the rickety Renault R4 owned by Liliana's friend César, whom Gisi already knew because he had gone to school with them. Running around a little by the river, swimming, playing ball, lying on the grass. Actually, it was like the old days, the long summer vacation, Christmas and New Years' Eve, which they spent together. They never argued. There were never even small disagreements, which are usually unavoidable when two people share a room for a long time and one of them is only a guest.

But something was different, says Liliana. Gisi had changed. She concentrated fully on only one thing, her cause. That was what was important to her and nothing else. Now and then Liliana tried to convince her to flee abroad — surely your parents will think of something, I'll talk to them, she said, which would not have been very difficult since Guillermo was their family doctor and Helga her gynecologist. She already served as a messenger between the parents and the daughter, but Gisi always offered the same answer: No, because then our struggle would have been in vain.

She did not say: our struggle, but: Alfredo's struggle. "Then Alfredo's struggle would have been in vain." Verbatim.

It was not only his struggle, it was a collective struggle, and you are one of the members of the collective. But you must also think of yourself. In fact, you have a duty to think of yourself. To save your life.

But Gisi did not want to discuss that.

One day in February she said, I have to move on.

Why, asked Liliana, you are safe here, no one will find you here.

It's better this way.

Liliana sensed — and knew that Gisi also sensed — that this would be a farewell for a long time. She watched her friend depart, standing tall and brave, with her bag over her shoulder and her hands free.

XXVII
Mendoza, Argentina
1976-1977

Do you remember José Galumba? He was the son of Czech immigrants who slaved away until they were too tired to enjoy their modest prosperity. He grew up in General Alvear, a small, dusty town in the southern part of the province. At the university in Mendoza he fell in love with Alicia, whose father was either a commissioned officer or a warrant officer in the reserves. She returned his love, the love of a boy, who for hours on end – even whole nights – kept still, drank *maté*, and said nothing. They married and had a daughter whom they named Natalia and a son, Mauricio. Before or perhaps between the births of his children José had broken off his studies and begun to deliver factory-made furniture to the home furnishing stores in Mendoza, San Juan, and San Luis.

The business was profitable, and they were able to rent a house that was large enough to accommodate two Montoneros besides themselves. Natalia was eighteen months old and Mauricio was seven months old when a commando stormed the house and abducted the children along with their mother. José narrowly escaped arrest; he was coming home and was about fifty meters from the house when he saw them. He turned around, crawled under the aqueduct of an irrigation channel, and fled the next day to San Juan. Because his wife's father still had contacts among his former comrades in the military, Alicia was imprisoned but not killed. Her parents were permitted to take in her daughter while Mauricio stayed with his mother in the cell she shared with prostitutes.

Six months after Alicia's arrest, at Christmas 1976, José wrote his children a thirty-eight-page letter in which he assured them "with the most heartfelt sentiments that a father is capable of and with the most tender of kisses" that he had not forgotten them and will never forget them and that in everything he does and has done he has acted for their personal happiness, which is inseparable from the common good. He described the preconditions of this nexus, with a guilty conscience, because his children were too young for his remarks, yet also with a confidence that one day they would understand him. In this context he used the words "equality," "justice," "freedom" (and contrast pairs such as rich man—poor man; money that creates money—hardship that produces more hardship; air travel—hunger; children's parties—ragpicking). Moreover, words like "monopoly," "religion," "exploitation," "extermination," "socialism," and "the people." He declared his love for their mother. He wrote that snow was falling the first time they kissed, thick, heavy flakes; that he had wrapped his jacket around Alicia's shoulders; that they had always made decisions together after talking things out and coming to an agreement; and that it nearly tore his heart out to be so powerless when the commando attacked them and their mother. He asked them to understand why he ran away, why he did not surrender, because it would not have helped, because that could not have saved them. Then once again the word "love," and for the first time the word "hope." Hope for a reunion, for the many kisses, for a life together, all four of them. But earlier in the letter, right in the middle, José had written that it was possible that he might not be alive when they read these lines "because I am part of society's contradictions and am fighting to overcome them."

By a circuitous route the letter reached José's parents, who wrapped it in an oilcloth, placed it in a can, and buried it behind the house. Two years later Alicia was released from prison, but just one week after being discharged she was arrested again. In 1980 she was finally set free and took custody of her children. For a long time they knew nothing of the letter. Only when his parents died, did José's siblings dare to unearth it. They gave it to his children who, a quarter century later, were skeptical yet touched by their legacy. For their part, Natalie and Mauricio now have children of their own, who are much older than they themselves were at that time, *hijos muy hermosos*, as Mili maintains, not only beautiful but also very compassionate young people. Mauricio, by the way, is said to be just as quiet as his father.

José had held out the longest in San Juan. One day in March 1977 he rang the Tenenbaums' doorbell on Calle Juan Jufré (it was pure coincidence that he found them there because on April 1 they were to move into an old house on Calle Coronel Díaz that they had been renovating for three months). He had come the entire way by foot, staying off the main routes, walking along sandy paths, and now he stood in front of Helga and Willi, sweaty, exhausted, and with a sack of hand grenades on his back.

The same night or the next day he was taken to the small apartment in Godoy Cruz, by you or by Ana María Moral.

Ana María, about whom I have been able to learn

precious little—her nickname, her last assumed identity, her particular swimming specialty, her age (25), her major (literary studies) and the name of her boyfriend (Luis Moyano), who was beaten to death by four or five policemen in San Juan in December 1976. Ana María had become pregnant by him and suffered a miscarriage in January. Helga attended to her medical needs, and Willi also cared for her. The two of them invited her to come along when they drove out into the countryside with you and Mónica. She joined them a few times, but then failed to show up one day. Her death occurred in the church, in a cell, or somewhere else. Her body was dumped into a shallow pit in a cemetery, in secrecy, but her parents learned how she perished and where her remains are located. That is where her grave is. And her name.

If you remain among us, then both what is said and what is left unsaid about you will linger. The desire to keep you alive as well as the need to be able to bury you.

What do I know that you don't know?

Mónica's recollection of your final meeting. At a campground, on the edge of a pool. The blackened hair, the half-closed eyes. The body, as solitary as a weather vane. The naked, scraped feet, the badly lacerated skin.

But why?

Because I have to run a lot.

Mónica on one side of the pool, you across from her. Your face, the lines of your body and your sadness. What unsettles her most is, why you had no survival instinct. It must have to do with depression or fanaticism, she'll say.

And the next to last image: the two of you wandering about for a long time, side by side. But you did not disclose anything to her, anything intimate that would have meant something to her alone. She maintains that you already had something of the soldier in you. Worse yet, you had transformed yourself into one. You were no longer Gisela Tenenbaum.

Even then, when Helga was so worried that she unwittingly exclaimed, what on earth am I going to do with you, Gisi! Should I dig a hole and hide you in it, deep in the ground, where they can't find you?

You laughed.

It was not a cynical laugh, nor a disheartened laugh. Rather it was a laugh of polite incomprehension, as if you couldn't grasp what Helga meant.

Whatever is she talking about?

That is the question that Mónica still asks herself: why you continued even when everything was lost. When Alfredo went missing, when you no longer had responsibility for others. Because you would not have found your way in everyday life? Because you thought that you had nothing left to lose? But you lost your family in doing so. And your family lost you. Your absence caused their silence.

Mónica kept silent because your father was silent (and she did not want to hurt him) and because she could not bring herself to speak of you as a dead person. Helga was the only one who would not let herself be beaten down. She wound a white kerchief around her head and demonstrated, for your life. Mónica didn't; she was afraid of meeting someone there who would tell her that you had been murdered. Her sister Gisela, whom she had considered invincible, omnipotent, who will liberate the poor from their poverty, who will overthrow the government, who will confer human rights upon humanity. In a later phase you seemed a monster to her, she says. She imagined your mutilated body just as they probably mutilated you: your chest lacerated, your arms mere stumps, and one eye gouged out. Then there was a period when, alone at home, she would panic because she constantly thought she heard you. Your voice, your footsteps, the creaking of the door that you open and close. She was also afraid that her fiancé's family would not accept her because of you. An insurgent's sister who wreaked God knows what kind of havoc! But above all she was unable to talk about you in the past tense.

That's over. She is more at peace with herself. She tries to believe with all her might that you will not come back. Until she is as strong as Heidi, whom it bothers that hardly anyone speaks to her about you. Mabel, for example, a friend, who was also your friend, with whom you played as a child, has never once inquired about you. Nor have Oscar's relatives. Years later Oscar said that they would ask him about her, behind Heidi's back because they wanted to spare your sister. How wonderfully tactful that they left her alone in her grief and distress!

Perhaps they had the wrong friends. Liliana, for example, asked your parents at every opportunity: Have you heard anything? Are there any new leads? She thinks that Helga and Guillermo aged ten or fifteen years overnight. She paid no attention to the rumors that you had been seen here or there. If they had been true, Mónica says, if you had survived, then you would have contacted her.

Or Miguel who only made it as far as Brazil with his wife and the other couple. They did not obtain a residency permit, and there was not enough money for the trip to France, so after six or seven months they gave up. Not until his return did Miguel hear that you were missing. He hoped that this rumor was just as groundless as the earlier one, that you had been shot in San Juan. He recalled her instruction to steer clear of your parents. He no longer felt himself so bound by it. Willi told him that the rumor was unfortunately true. Years passed. Miguel was promoted to head of quality control and then to a post as technical director at a cement factory. Once he ran into Willi on a flight from Mendoza to Buenos Aires. He asked him whether there were any new developments. Your father shook his head.

Miguel thinks that the worst part is that no one can even bring you flowers. Because they don't know where to place them. He hopes that there will be justice someday, justice as well as certainty, about where you are and what remains of you. Your parents want nothing more than to learn what happened to you, says Paola, who still cherishes your present, the red teddy bear.

If they could just find one of your bones, lay it to rest, and with it the pain, and scatter flowers in your honor. Then they would be able to die in peace, but please not too soon, and not untimely.

XXVIII

Recently, Helga was berating herself: if only I had . . . ! If only Gisi and I had . . . ! To which Paola responded, Gisi lived the way she wanted to. She did what she thought was right, and no one could have persuaded her otherwise. She chose her path freely and with full knowledge of the risks. She was not coerced into anything. She never backed down.

Again and again I tell myself, that was her path. But that's still no comfort to me.

Made in the USA
Lexington, KY
02 December 2014